STUDIES IN ENGLISH LITERATURE

Volume XX

SOUND AND SENSE
IN
DYLAN THOMAS'S POETRY

by

LOUISE BAUGHAN MURDY

1966

MOUTON & CO.

THE HAGUE · PARIS

Printed in The Netherlands by Mouton & Co., Printers, The Hague.

To my parents
who first taught me to love
the spoken and the written word

ACKNOWLEDGMENTS

It is impossible to acknowledge my indebtedness to all the corporations and to all the people that enabled me to publish this book. I could not even have launched upon so ambitious an academic undertaking as the doctoral program without the assistance of a three-year Southern Fellowships Fund grant. And I could not have carried out the necessary research without the help of the Interlibrary Loan Department of the University of Florida. Since this book developed from my dissertation, I am especially indebted to Dr. Ants Oras for a combination of kindness and criticism which makes for an outstanding research director. I wish to express my appreciation to Dr. Stephen F. Fogle, Dr. John T. Fain, Dr. T. Walter Herbert, and Dr. Louisa Duls, who read the manuscript and made invaluable suggestions. From Professor John Malcolm Brinnin, Professor Gene Baro, Professor Daniel G. Hoffman, Mr. Lloyd Frankenberg, Dr. Arthur L. Klein, Professor W. T. Weathers, Professor Clifton C. Hill, and Mr. James E. Hansen, among others, I have received information of a technical nature. I am, above all, everlastingly grateful to my husband for his understanding, encouragement — and patience.

TABLE OF CONTENTS

INTRODUCTION

Over the years, criticism of Dylan Thomas's poetry has generally emphasized either its sound *or* its sense. On the one hand, critics who disparage Thomas contend that sound dominates his poetry almost to the exclusion of sense. John Wain, for example, comments that a set of meanings can be extracted from Thomas's poems but that it is doubtful whether or not Thomas really cared much about any precise meaning as long as the sound of the poem satisfied him.[1] Even more vitriolic in his condemnation of Thomas's poetry is Robert Graves, who writes:

Dylan Thomas was drunk with melody, and what the words were he cared not. He was eloquent, and what cause he was pleading, he cared not. ... He kept musical control of the reader without troubling about the sense.[2]

On the other hand, critics like Elder Olson and Derek Stanford, who admire and defend Thomas, attempt expositions of the sense of his poems. Few studies other than the excellent articles by William T. Moynihan try to relate sound and sense in Thomas's poetry. The method of this study is to submit analyses of certain aspects of the sound patterns in twenty-eight selected examples of Dylan Thomas's poetry and to relate these aspects of sound to the sense of his poetry.

There is no doubt that Thomas himself felt that auditory effects contribute to the total meaning of a poem. To understand and

[1] See "Dylan Thomas: A Review of his *Collected Poems*", in *Preliminary Essays* (New York, 1957), p. 182.
[2] *The Crowning Privilege: Collected Essays on Poetry* (New York, 1956), pp. 138-139.

appreciate both sound and sense, he believed, one should read a poem silently under conditions that allow concentrated time for study and assessment and, whenever possible, one should read a poem orally, or at least read it silently as if he were reading it orally.[3] Silent reading is private reading, and oral reading is often public reading. In this connection, Thomas said that the printed page is the place in which to examine the works of a poem, the platform the place in which to give the poem "the works".[4] Upon other occasions Thomas more seriously expressed his belief in the importance of oral reading of poetry. In a B.B.C. broadcast of 1946, he defined poetry as

memorable words-in-cadence which move and excite me emotionally. And, once you've got the hang of it, it should always be better when read aloud than when read silently with the eyes. Always.[5]

Six years later, in a conference held by Thomas with students at the University of Utah, he commented upon the value of oral reading in helping the listener to interpret the total meaning of the poem. As Thomas said, oral reading of poetry brings the listener closer to the poet. It follows, then, that a poet's reading of his own poems usually brings one closest to the poet and to his intended emphases and interpretations.

Thomas's sincerity in his belief that sound is an important component in the total meaning of a poem is further emphasized by the fact that he read his poetry orally. Thus he did not leave to the printed page the interpretation of his poetry. Through oral reading, he was — to an unusually high degree — able to communicate to the audience the total meaning of his poetry. He had such an acute sense of gesture, volume, timing, and intonation that to the listener his performances seemed to be an expressive, spontaneous melody. But his talents carried an inherent weakness, which Thomas recognized: he was unable to read well poetry that is restrained and intellectual. Most of the time, however, Thomas

---

[3] See "Dylan Thomas on Reading his Poetry: introduction to a poetry reading", *Mademoiselle*, XLII (July, 1956), p. 37.
[4] *Idem.*
[5] Dylan Thomas, James Stephens, and Gerald Bullet, "On poetry: A Discussion", *Encounter*, III (November, 1954), p. 23.

was free to choose the selections he read, and he chose to read only the poets he liked. He himself said:

And when I read aloud the poems of modern poets I like very much, I try to make them alive from inside. I try to get across what I feel, however wrongly, to be the original impetus of the poem. I am a practicing interpreter, however much of a flannel-tongued one-night-stander.[6]

Although Thomas asserted that he disliked reading his own poems in public, his readings of them were even more an interpretation and re-creation than were his readings of other poets' works. Perhaps Thomas's hesitancy to read his own poems stemmed from his realization of the dangers of a poet's reading his own works.[7] In introducing a reading of his own poems he once explained:

[But the danger] for what a reader-aloud of his own poems so often does, is to mawken or melodramatise them, making a single, simple phrase break with the fears or throb with the terrors from which he deludes himself the phrase has been born.

There is the other reader, of course, who manages, by studious flatness, semidetachment, and an almost condescending undersaying of his poems, to give the impression that what he really means is: Great things, but my own.[8]

Thomas further remarked that the suspected weaknesses of a poem are often confirmed when the author reads his work. Despite his concern for the problems involved, Thomas did read well many of his own poems. As John Lehmann said, with Thomas "more than with any other poet of our time, the voice heightened and illuminated the power of the word".[9]

[6] "Dylan Thomas on Reading his Poetry: introduction to a poetry reading", p. 37.
[7] Thomas was certainly sensitive in his criticism of *other* people's oral reading of his poetry. Once when a verse-speaking choir recited "And death shall have no dominion" to him over the telephone, he described the reading to Vernon Watkins as "Picked voices picking the rhythm to bits, chosen elocutionists choosing their own meanings, ten virgins weeping slowly over a quick line, matrons mooing the refrain, a conductor with all his vowels planed to the last e." *Letters to Vernon Watkins* (New York, 1957), p. 50. (Hereafter this volume will be abbreviated to *LVW*.)
[8] *Quite Early One Morning* (Norfolk, Conn., 1954), p. 167.
[9] In E. W. Tedlock, *Dylan Thomas: The Legend and the Poet* (London, 1960), p. 47. Thomas is one of the few modern poets to have become known first through his recordings and only later through his printed poems. Americans

Thomas even went so far in his emphasis on the importance of sound to the total meaning of a poem that his poems were sometimes shaped by oral reading. Sometimes he began composing a poem merely on the basis of a single resonant, pregnant phrase which suggested another phrase, which reinforced and elaborated the original phrase. As one phrase suggested another phrase, Thomas read his poetry aloud to himself, criticized it, and altered it. Although he has been attacked for "an unbalanced delight in the mere sound of words",[10] he denied being more interested in sound than in sense.[11]

Certainly Thomas did very deliberately utilize devices of rhyme, rhythm, and word-formation. As he explained in his "Poetic Manifesto" of 1951:

I am a painstaking, conscientious, involved and devious craftsman in words, however unsuccessful the result so often appears, and to whatever wrong uses I may apply my techical [sic] paraphenalia. I use everything & anything to make my poems work and move in the direction I want them to: old tricks, new tricks, puns, portmanteau-words, paradox, allusion, paronomasia, paragram, catachresis, slang, assonantal rhymes, vowel rhymes, sprung rhythm. Every device there is in language is there to be used if you will.[12]

But, Thomas did not alter portions of a poem purely for the sake of the sound; his best poetry reveals more than a mere "lovely gift of the gab". Indeed he once accused Vernon Watkins of making criticisms on the basis of sound rather than of total meaning:

I think you are liable, in your criticism of me, to underrate the value — or, rather, the integrity, the wholeness — of what I am saying or trying to make clear that I am saying, and often to suggest alterations or amendments for purely musical motives.[13]

Although Thomas is not — like T. S. Eliot, for example — an

---

first acclaimed Thomas as a result of his recordings with Caedmon Publishers. In fact, the struggling new Caedmon company became successful largely as a result of the popularity of Thomas's readings. By 1962 the U.S. public had bought 400,000 copies of various recordings of Dylan Thomas reading Dylan Thomas.

[10] Geoffrey Bullough, *The Trend of Modern Poetry* (London, 1949), pp. 219-220.

[11] See Babette Deutsch, *Poetry in Our Time* (New York, 1956), p. 331.

[12] *Texas Quarterly*, IV (Winter, 1961), p. 50.

[13] *LVW*, p. 66.

intellectual poet, his poetry does, of course, have "meaning", but, especially in the later poetry, the total meaning is more *mood* or *emotion* than *thought*. At all times Thomas had the need to *feel* the effectiveness of his poetry.[14] He wanted a poem "to do more than just to have the appearance of 'having been created' ";[15] he wanted it to be a "fresh imagining".[16] He strived to achieve "the strong, inevitable pulling that makes a poem an event, a happening, an action perhaps, not a still-life or experience put down, placed, regulated".[17] And in his best poems Thomas does express incontrovertible, living truths. Within the framework of the total meaning, then, Thomas attempts to balance sound and sense. For the ideal relationship between sound and sense in poetry of the highest excellence follows Pope's famous dictum that "The sound must seem an Echo to the sense". In such great poetry — among which Thomas's best deserves place — sound is a medium of sense.

Because this book concerns the sound of poetry, because Thomas himself stressed the importance of oral reading of poetry, and because an author's own reading of his poetry illuminates its meaning, the poems under analysis are limited to the twenty-eight poems recorded by Thomas and available on commercial records or on the University of Florida tape.[18] These twenty-eight poems constitute almost one-third of Thomas's ninety-one *Collected Poems*.

In order to show the development of sound and sense in Thomas's

---

[14]   Several examples can readily be cited from Thomas's letters to Vernon Watkins. In connection with Watkins's criticism of a line in "Twenty-four years", Thomas said: "And sorry about that bracketed line in the birthday poem, but, until I can think of something else or feel, it will have to stay." (*LVW*, p. 49.) In a similar instance concerning "Once it was the colour of saying", Thomas explained: "I see your argument about the error of shape, but the form was consistently emotional and I can't change it without a change of heart." (*LVW*, p. 54.)

[15]   *LVW*, p. 38.

[16]   *Ibid.*, p. 39.

[17]   *Ibid.*, p. 38.

[18]   After this study was completed, Caedmon released the album *Dylan Thomas Reading his Complete Recorded Poetry*, with five poems which were not available on earlier commercial recordings or on the University of Florida tape. For commentary on this album, see the Thomas Discography, footnote 4.

poetry, it is necessary to discuss his poetic periods. Thomas's
poetic output varies in quantity — as well as in quality — during
his three poetic periods. The length of each period is nearly the
same: the first period covers five years, the second period six years,
and the third period seven years. But of the poems later published
in *Collected Poems*, Thomas wrote seven times as many in the first
poetic period as he wrote in the third poetic period. More specifically, in his early poetic period (1933-1938), he published fifty-four
of the poems in *Collected Poems*; in his middle poetic period
(1939-1945), he published twenty-nine of these poems; and in his
late poetic period (1946-1953), he published only eight of these
poems. Since Thomas was somewhat hesitant about reading his
own poetry in public and since he chose with particular care those
selections he did read, it is not surprising that a higher percentage
of the poems he wrote in his middle and late — and better and more
mature — poetic periods are recorded by him than poems he wrote
in his early poetic period. Quite naturally, he read those works he
judged his best. The poems under consideration in this study repre-
sent about one-fifth of the poems in *Collected Poems* which Thomas
wrote in his early period, about two-fifths of those he wrote in his
middle period, and three-fourths of those he wrote in his late period.

Each of the three periods of Thomas's poetry will be described
in greater detail in the chapter devoted to the poems of that period.
It is necessary here to say only that these categories, although valid
as outlines for the development of sound and sense in Thomas's
poetry, are not designed as watertight compartments. The characteristics of adjacent periods necessarily overlap. Yet their general
validity was recognized by Thomas himself, as recorded by William
York Tindall.[19]

The three chapters of this book consider, respectively, Thomas's
three poetic periods. The twenty-eight poems under examination
are arranged chronologically by date of revision — where applicable
— or by date of composition.[20] The ten poems discussed in the
first chapter are:

[19]   See "Burning and Crested Song", *American Scholar*, XXII (Autumn, 1953),
pp. 488-489.
[20]   The chronology follows the listing by Ralph N. Maud in "Dylan Thomas'

The twelve poems discussed in the second chapter are:

The six poems discussed in the third chapter are:

Collected Poems: Chronology of Composition", *PMLA*, LXXVI (June, 1961), pp. 292-297. It would be advantageous for the reader of the commentaries to refer to each poem as it is discussed. Appendix III is an alphabetized index of Dylan Thomas's *Collected Poems* which will facilitate the reader in finding a poem in either the Dent or the New Directions editions.

The purpose of this book is to reveal — through an analysis of the relationship between sound and sense in the twenty-eight selected poems from the three poetic periods — Thomas's poetic development toward an expansive poetry in which sound supports sense and contributes to the total meaning. The analysis of each poem involves a consideration of two poetic components closely related to sound and sense:

(1) prosodic structure — syllabic patterns, speech-stress patterns, paragraph or stanza formation, line-end word patterns, distribution of pauses

(2) auditory repetitions and links, especially in arrangements of vowel and consonantal sounds. (Throughout the study, references to vowel and consonantal sounds use the symbols of the International Phonetic Alphabet.[21])

Thomas's poetic development is, fundamentally, from an earlier poetry that is staccato in its rhythm and compressed — sometimes obscure — in its sense, to a later poetry that is legato in its rhythm and expansive — often uncomplicated — in its sense. Thomas

[21]

	Symbol	Pronunciation	Symbol	Pronunciation
Vowels:	i	bee	ʊ	full
	ɪ	pity	u	tooth
	e	rate	ɝ	fur*ther*
	ɛ	yet	ɚ	furth*er*
	æ	sang	ə	*a*bove
	a	far	ʌ	ab*o*ve
	ɔ	jaw		
	o	go		
Diphthongs:	aɪ	while	ɔɪ	toy
	aʊ	how	ɪu	fuse
Consonants:	p	pie	h	how
	b	bee	tʃ	wa*tch*
	t	too	dʒ	jaw
	d	d*o*	m	mow
	k	cut	n	now
	g	go	ŋ	sa*ng*
	f	*f*ull	l	fu*ll*
	v	*v*ision	w	*w*atch
	θ	too*th*	hw	*wh*ile
	ð	fur*th*er	j	*y*et
	s	*s*ang	r	*r*ate
	z	u*s*ing	ʃ	di*sh*
	ʒ	vi*s*ion		

referred to his poetry as "the record of my individual struggle from darkness towards some measure of light",[22] and certainly the total meaning of his poetry does progress from the darkness of self-concern and fear to the light of faith and love. (Perhaps Thomas was expressing his expanded vision when he wrote in "Ceremony After a Fire Raid" that "Love is the last light spoken".) Among the tendencies which contribute to the general contrast between the earlier and later poetry are the shift in structure from relatively end-stopped units to longer grammatical units, the shift in phonetic atmosphere from a striking use of explosives to a more subtle use of continuants, and the shift toward increasingly intricate and pervasive designs of auditory repetitions and of syllabic and speech-stress patterns.

Of course this study cannot exhaust the possibilities even of the limited aspects of sound and sense which are explored. A complete study would probably be so complex as to break down under its own machinery. Although scientific methods can be used for purposes of analysis, poetry itself is no science. Formulas cannot create poetry of high excellence. When asked for the rules of poetry, Thomas replied that there weren't any, that a poet made his own rules, and that the result either was or wasn't poetry.[23] Some of the subtlest and loveliest auditory effects, indeed, escape analysis. Although Thomas was a dedicated craftsman, he believed poetry to be ultimately a sublime enigma:

You can tear a poem apart to see what makes it technically tick, and say to yourself when the works are laid out before you, the vowels, the consonants, the rhymes and rhythms, Yes, this is it, this is why the poem moves me so. It is because of the craftsmanship. But you're back again where you began. The best craftsmanship always leaves holes and gaps in the works of the poems so that something that is not in the poem can creep, crawl, flash or thunder in.[24]

[22] *Quite Early One Morning*, p. 188.
[23] See Caitlin Thomas, *Leftover Life to Kill* (New York, 1957), p. 69.
[24] "Dylan Thomas on Reading his Poetry: introduction to a poetry reading", p. 37.

CHAPTER I

The following chapter analyzes sound and sense in ten of the poems from Thomas's most prolific and experimental period, 1933 to 1939:

     I – "From love's first fever to her plague"
    II – "Light breaks where no sun shines"
   III – "If I were tickled by the rub of love"
   IV – "Especially when the October wind"
    V – "The hand that signed the paper"
   VI – "Should lanterns shine"
  VII – "And death shall have no dominion"
 VIII – "It is the sinners' dust-tongued bell"
   IX – "After the Funeral"
    X – "When all my five and country senses see"

Before analyzing each poem, it seems advantageous to mention the characteristics of this whole period. The chief quality of the poems of Thomas's first poetic period — in contrast with the quality of Thomas's later poems — is their compressed meaning. Moreover, the themes of the early poems arise from opposites, notably the "womb-tomb" themes. Thomas himself best explains his method of obtaining an effect of compression by using conflicting images:

I let an image be made emotionally in me and then apply to it what intellectual and critical force I possess; let it breed another; let that image contradict the first; make of the third image out of the other two together, a fourth contradictory image, and let them all, within my imposed formal limits, conflict. ... The life in any poem of mine cannot move concentrically round a central image, the life must come out of the centre; an image must be born and die in another; and any sequence of my images must be a sequence of creations, recreations, destructions, contradictions.[1]

Another characteristic of this first period is that sound patterns less frequently than in later periods correlate significantly with sense; when they do correlate significantly, it is often in only a phrase or line. And the general auditory pattern is of a staccato rhythm, enhanced by a predominance of striking explosives, by a tendency toward metrical regularity, by characteristically end-stopped lines, and by obvious rather than subtle auditory repetitions. In short, the early poems tend to be compressed and "obscure" in meaning, striking but obvious in sound.

I

"From love's first fever to her plague" seems, at first glance, as if it might be throughout rather smooth and light in rhythm. The syllabic pattern is quite irregular; the lines are varied, from four to thirteen syllables; the line-end word patterns reveal no significant assonance or consonance; the paragraph formation ranges from three to nine lines in a paragraph. In themselves these characteristics could contribute to a fluid rhythm.

Other elements than the above combine, however, to make the rhythm predominantly slow, if not sometimes heavy. The speech-stress patterns[2] generally tend toward the iambic and, in paragraph VI, are almost perfectly iambic:

> I 'learnt the 'verbs of 'will, and 'had my 'secret;
> The 'code of 'night 'tapped on my 'tongue;
> What 'had been 'one was 'many 'sounding 'minded.

The syntactical repetitions (the numerous phrases beginning with "from" and the phrases "One womb, one mind", "One breast", and "One sun, one manna") and the echoes ("Shone in my ears

---

[1] C. Day-Lewis, *The Poetic Image* (New York, 1947), p. 122.
[2] Throughout the study the speech-stress patterns are based on Thomas's speech stresses in his recorded readings of his poetry.

the light of sound, / Called in my eyes the sound of light") are obvious auditory links. There is a high frequency of pauses:[3] twenty-two occur within lines and thirty-eight occur at line ends. Because nearly 80 per cent of the lines conclude with the finality of a comma or period, it is not surprising that most of the lines end in weighty words, many of which are nouns. (Indeed, most of these nouns are stressed monosyllables.) It is interesting to note that every paragraph terminates in a period.

The poem concerns the evolution of a poet from the simplicity of innocent childhood to the complexity of bewildered adolescence to the simplicity-in-complexity of mature manhood.[4] To a certain extent the poem's phonetics shift to reinforce the shift in meaning. That is, the opening paragraphs seem smooth and light when compared with the slower, heavier, later paragraphs. In the opening paragraphs the voiced continuants frequently produce a soft, lingering effect; in the later paragraphs the explosives frequently produce a sharp, clipped effect.

The apparent simplicity of infancy is reflected in the predominant monosyllables and the simple balance and repetition of the lines descriptive of man's earliest years. In the phrase "All world was one, one windy nothing", alliteration and assonance are obvious in the five *w* sounds, three *n* sounds, two *l* sounds, and three *ʌ* sounds. The singleness of a child's vision is emphasized by the repetition of the word "one" in that phrase and in the closing lines of the stanza:

> And earth and sky were as one airy hill,
> The sun and moon shed one white light.

The simple sound pattern of two internal rhymes within one line ("sun", "one" and "white", "light") reinforces the meaning. Part of the melodiousness of the line results from the almost continuous alternation between vowel (or semivowel) and consonant in these two lines. The exceptions to this alternation are climaxed by the

---

[3] Throughout the study the term "pauses" refers to any punctuation mark in the poetry which designates an interval of silence.
[4] Such a cyclical theme is common in Thomas, who (like William Blake) seems to have believed that without contraries there can be no progression.

final stop *t*, repeated twice, and the initial labial *l* in the strong, slow phrase "white light".

The final lines of stanzas I and II form closely related lines placed in inverted order:

> And earth and sky were as one airy hill,
> The sun and moon shed one white light.
> . . . .
> The sun was red, the moon was grey,
> The earth and sky were as two mountains meeting.

A noteworthy aspect of the sound structure of these four related lines is that, in the speech-stressed syllables, the patterns of the striking power and the vowel tone are relatively parallel. Since these patterns move in the same direction, they reinforce each other's audibility. For "The sun and moon shed one white light" is an emotionally charged line in which the crescendo builds to two final words of high and almost identical power and of identical tone: "white light".

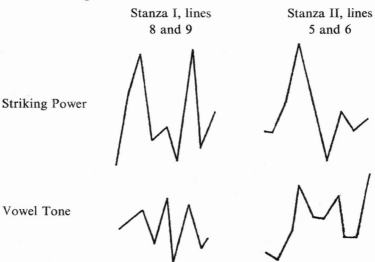

Stanza I, lines
8 and 9

Stanza II, lines
5 and 6

Striking Power

Vowel Tone

In later paragraphs the complexity of adolescent and adult life is often echoed in the profusion of explosives, such as in the lines "The roo*t* of *t*ongues en*d*s in a s*p*en*t*-ou*t* *c*ancer, / Tha*t* *b*u*t* a name, where ma*ggo*ts have their X [*cross*]." The concept of the slow, painful process of reaching maturity is reinforced by the assonantal wail in "*wi*se to the cr*y*ing th*i*gh". The feelings of harshness of life are reflected in consecutive stressed monosyllables and the insistent alliteration of "Need no word's warmth".

In general, then, the sound in "From love's first fever to her plague" reflects the sense in that the impression of the opening paragraphs is of relative simplicity and the impression of the later paragraphs is of relative complexity. In the opening paragraphs continuants and vowels are more prominent, and in the later paragraphs explosives and consonantal clusters become more conspicuous.

II

"Light breaks where no sun shines" is a deliberate and forceful poem. Its five stanzas are composed of six lines each, in regular syllabic verse with a sustained pattern:

Stanza	Number of Syllables in Each Line
I	6 10 4 10 4 10
II	6 10 4 10 4 10
III	6 10 4 10 4 10
IV	6 10 4 10 4 10
V	6 10 4 10 *6* 10

Although no definite pattern of speech stresses appears, scattered occurrences of consecutive stressed monosyllables seem outstanding. And, stressed or unstressed, the words of the poem are, in about nine out of ten cases, monosyllables. Another factor contributing to the forcefulness of "Light breaks" is that one out of every six syllables is of high striking power. No other poem under consideration has proportionately so many syllables of high striking power. And these syllables occur, interestingly enough, in an initial position in one out of every three lines and in a terminal position in one out of every three lines. As for the pauses in the poem, three-fourths of the lines are end-stopped, with all the paragraphs ending with a period. Such a balanced and emphasized structure helps create an insistent rhythmic effect.

Thomas's realization of the importance of sound to the total meaning of a poem is reflected in the very method of composition of many of his poems. For sometimes he built a poem of sound and sense from a single phrase which haunted him. Witness his statements in *Letters to Vernon Watkins* concerning the following phrases: "when I woke the dawn spoke", the inspiration for the poem by that title[5]; "I advance for as long as forever is", the inspiration for "Twenty-four years"[6]; and "desireless familiar", the inspiration for "To Others than You".[7] In fact, the phrase "where no sun shines" may well have formed the nucleus for "Light breaks", particularly since only a month before writing this poem Thomas had used similar word-order in two phrases in "From love's first fever to her plague": "When no mouth stirred" (I, 5) and "who ... Need no word's warmth" (V, 6).

Although Thomas's method of composition probably cannot be substantiated — since, according to Ralph N. Maud, the MS. version for "Light breaks where no sun shines" shows few if any variants — it is indisputable that the phrase is the syntactical basis of the poem. In stanza I occur "where no sun shines", "Where no sea runs", and "where no flesh decks the bones". Thereafter the repetitions occur with diminishing frequency: in Stanza II, "Where no seed stirs: and "Where no wax is"; in stanza IV, "Where no cold is". These consecutive stressed monosyllables hammer a steady, strong rhythm.

Like the syntactical repetitions, other aspects of the organization of this poem are also more deliberate and obvious in the opening stanzas than in the succeeding ones. For example, in both stanza I and stanza II lines 1, 3, 4, and 6 end in a *z* sound; in the succeeding stanzas a final *z* or *s* sound at the end of the line occurs irregularly. Throughout the poem a large percentage of the words terminate with a sibilant. Indeed such a prominence of sibilants may reveal that Thomas's early experimentation with correlating or contrasting

⁵   P. 41.
⁶   P. 48.
⁷   P. 68.

sound and meaning is not always successful.[8] In an informally taped
recording — made in Gainesville, Florida, in 1950, with only his
host, Gene Baro, present — Thomas mars this poem with four
small misreadings, all involving the final *s* sound.[9] Naturally such
minor misreadings are insignificant in themselves, but they do
indicate that even Thomas himself found the frequent occurrence
of sibilants somewhat confusing.

The variety of relationships among the line-end words merits
attention. The predominance of final consonance (of sibilants) has
already been discussed. Initial consonance occurs in "heart",
"heads"; "rounds", "robes". Assonance occurs in "shines", "tides",
"light"; "bone", "robes", "globes"; "unpin", "lids". Initial and
final consonance occur in "stirs", "stars". Full rhyme occurs in
"robes", "globes"; "die", "eye". Of the internal auditory effects
one of the most suggestive occurs in the line "Div*i*ning in a sm*i*le the
o*i*l of tears." With assonance linked with approximate rhyme, the
phrase glides smoothly. The final word, "tears", is the only
important word omitted from this linkage, and its isolation helps
to point out the semantic contrast between "smile" and "tears".

According to most interpretations, the chief concern of "Light
breaks" is sexual activity which leads to the conception of new life.
The prospect of new life "where no sun shines" seems viewed with
hope, even though death is implicit in life.[10] But in the final line the
point of emphasis shifts suddenly; Thomas refers here not to the
fulfilled but to the *un*fulfilled sexual activity — i.e., the "waste
allotments", or sperm, which will not fertilize. Over these the sun,
the source of life and death, will never rise; "the dawn halts".
Because it bears the concluding and perhaps unexpected observation
of the poem, the final line is extremely important:

> Above the waste allotments the dawn halts.

The strong emotional effect of the line is influenced by t he skillfu

---

[8]   One successful use of the sibilants — in conjunction with the *t* sound — is
discussed below.

[9]   Thomas reads "seas run" for *Collected Poems* "sea runs", "socket" for *C.P.*
"sockets", "limits" for *C.P.* "limit", and "allotment" for *C.P.* "allotments".

[10]   That line 5 — "And blood jumps in the sun" — concludes this main thematic
development of the poem is accentuated by the fact that it is the only irregularity
in the syllabic pattern of the poem. It is lengthened from four to six syllables

use of combinations of *s* and *t*. For, sound reinforces meaning as
the line itself halts with harsh consonantal clusters: "wa*ste*", "allo*t*-
men*ts*", "hal*ts*". Moreover, the spondee of the monosyllables
"dawn halts" — especially since it follows the long, relatively fluid
"allotments" — creates a marked staccato rhythm. And the sharp
fall of the tone of the line and the assonance of the two final words
("dawn halts") contribute to the singular effectiveness of the poem's
conclusion.

III

In "If I were tickled by the rub of love" the poet wonders what
should be the ultimate consideration in his life and poetry. Basically
the treatment of the theme revolves upon a serious pun. With
reference to Hamlet's fifth soliloquy, the "rub" is the obstacle
causing fear of death. But Thomas, like the Queen in *Richard II*,
feels that "the world is full of rubs". He is concerned with a rub (a
friction) that will tickle one to forget, at least for the present, the
problem of death.

In the opening stanza the phonetic atmosphere revolves around
the predominant consonant of the thematically most important
word: "tickle". The explosive *k* and its cognate sound *g* echo
throughout the stanza: "roo*k*ing", "*g*irl", "Bro*k*e", "brea*k*ing",
"*c*attle", "*c*alve", "s*c*ratch". Other explosives emphasize the
auditory links: "ru*b*", "si*d*e", "*b*an*d*age*d*", "re*d*", "se*t*", "a*pp*le",
"floo*d*", "*b*a*d*", "*b*loo*d*", "s*p*ring". These consonants — particularly
the unvoiced ones (*p*, *t*, *k*) — produce a clipped, staccato effect.

In succeeding stanzas Thomas implies that if true love existed
for him he would be able to meet the prospect of death. Since the
world is imperfect ("half the devil's and my own"), perfect love
seems unattainable, and the forces of decay and death continuously
worm their way into life. As Thomas expresses it with a brilliant
and characteristic pun on "quick" as "life" or "living":[11]

> I sit and watch the worm beneath my nail
> Wearing the quick away.[12]

[11] Such a meaning of "quick" is familiar in the phrase "the quick and the dead".
[12] A more obvious instance of Thomas's use of "quick" as "living" is in

The poet understands that this life-in-death situation is true reality, "the only rub that tickles". Yet his conclusion is remarkably hopeful, for he decides that in his life and poetry he "would be tickled by the rub that is: / Man be my metaphor". In this final phrase the skillful use of alliteration (in "*M*an", "*m*y", "*m*etaphor") and of a polysyllable as a line-end word contributes to a strong and memorable closing.

This poem is not, however, among Thomas's more successful pieces. Although several phrases have brilliance, the clarity and depth of meaning and the consistency of approach throughout the poem leave something to be desired. Perhaps part of the weakness of the poem lies in the strict but relatively functionless regularity of the form. There are seven stanzas of seven lines each in syllabic verse of the following pattern:

Stanza	Number of Syllables in Each Line
I	10 10 10 10 10 10 6
II	10 10 10 10 10 10 6
III	*11* 10 10 *11* 10 10 6
IV	10 10 10 10 10 10 6
V	10 10 10 10 10 10 6
VI	*11* 10 10 *11* 10 10 6
VII	10 10 10 10 10 10 6

And the seeming exceptions to the pattern — the four instances of eleven syllables — are actually in identical positions in their respective stanzas. Further, the eleventh syllable in each case results from a feminine ending. Throughout the entire poem the final word of each line is a monosyllable except in these four cases and in the final line, "Man be my metaphor". Although there are few internal pauses, most of the lines are end-stopped, and all the paragraphs conclude with a period. The relationship between the line-end words, however, prevents the ends of the lines from seeming over-emphasized. The line-end words do not rhyme, except in the instances of "string", "spring" and "own", "bone." Instead, in the first six stanzas, final consonance occurs in the line-end words, in the pattern of *abcacbc*.

"A Winter's Tale", VI, 4, where he substitutes for the proverbial "in the dead of night", "in the quick of night".

I	lo*v*e, cal*v*e	IV	ru*b*, cri*b*
	si*d*e, floo*d*		lo*ck*, bro*k*e
	stri*ng*, lu*ng*, spri*ng*		jaw*s*, flie*s*, toe*s*
II	ce*lls*, hee*ls*	V	ow*n*, bo*n*e
	flesh, axe		gir*l*, nai*l*
	hai*r*, thigh, wa*r*		eye, sea, away
III	finge*rs*, hunge*rs*	VI	tickles, chuckle
	me*n*, loi*n*		se*x*, si*x*
	lo*v*e, ner*v*e, gra*v*e		twi*st*, brea*st*, du*st*

Exceptions occur in II *b* and *c*, in V *c* (where final vowels replace final consonants), and in VI *a*. The final stanza is quite irregular and contains only vestiges of the pattern of final consonance.

"If I were tickled by the rub of love" provides an interesting study of Thomas's early craftsmanship. For in its marked use of end-stopped lines, of syntactical repetitions ("If I were tickled by the ..."), of serious puns, and of explosives, the poem is typical of his early period.

IV

"Especially when the October wind" is one of the finest of Thomas's early achievements. His technique of immediacy is partially responsible for the poem's success. A metaphoric structure is utilized to communicate poetically the narrator's experiences, for Thomas describes the poet's visual and auditory perceptions on a particular October day in the terminology of poetic language: "syllabic blood", wordy shapes of women", "vowelled beeches", "water's speeches", "meadow's signs", "the signal grass", and "dark-vowelled birds".

The imagery of the poem is both visual and auditory. The visual image of "the rows / Of the star-gestured children in the park" vividly suggests the playing youngsters who, with arms and legs outstretched in uncontrolled abandon, momentarily resemble pointed stars. And the auditory image of "The spider-tongued, and the loud hill of Wales" is only one illustration of the "autumnal spells" which culminate in the final line of the poem: "By the sea's side hear the dark-vowelled birds." The absence of consonantal clusters, the alliteration ("sea's side"), and the assonance ("By", "side") enhance the smooth roll of the rhythm in the final line.

"Especially when the October wind" has many of the same characteristics as "If I were tickled by the rub of love". It is regular in form, with four stanzas of eight lines each. It is almost regular in syllabic pattern:[13]

Stanza	Number of Syllables in Each Line							
I	10	10	10	10	10	10	10	10
II	10	10	10	10	10	10	10	*11*
III	10	10	*11*	10	10	10	10	10
IV	10	10	10	10	10	*11*	*11*	9

It has syntactical repetitions — namely, "Some let me make you of ...." In the line-end words the final consonance forms a definite pattern (*abbacddc*):

I	wi*nd*, la*nd*	III	clo*ck*, co*ck*
	hai*r*, fire		meani*ng*, morni*ng*
	bir*ds*, wor*ds*		si*gns*, si*ns*
	sti*cks*, tal*ks*		know, eye
II	ma*rk*, pa*rk*	IV[14]	wi*nd*, la*nd*
	trees, rows		spe*lls*, Wa*les*
	bee*ches*, spee*ches*		wor*ds*, bir*ds*
	roo*ts*, no*tes*		scurry, fury

Sometimes the similarity between the pairs is complete rhyme, as in "birds", "words"; "mark", "park"; "beeches", "speeches"; "clock", "cock". Occasionally the similarity is between the initial *and* final consonants, as in "sins" and "signs" and (with the exception of the medial consonant *r*, which Thomas de-emphasized) in "meaning" and "morning". Also like "If I were tickled by the rub of love", the poem has numerous end-stopped lines. But the only complete pauses in the poem (i.e., the period punctuation marks) occur at

[13]   Unlike "If I were tickled by the rub of love", the deviations from the syllabic pattern in "Especially when the October wind" do not in themselves form a minor pattern caused by feminine endings.

[14]   Note that the first and last stanzas are linked not only by identical opening lines, but also by two sets of identical line-end words: "wind", "land", and "words", "birds".

the ends of lines and, primarily, at the ends of lines 4 and 8 of a
stanza. Combined with the line-end word pattern of final consonance, the pause pattern helps to link the four-line units together.

Yet "Especially when the October wind" *seems* less regular and
more subtle than most of Thomas's earlier poems. In part the
difference arises from the more continuous and prominent visual
and auditory imagery and from the swifter rhythm. In general,
the poem has fewer consonantal clusters, more semivowels
("wordy ... women", "windy weather", "wormy winter", among
others), and more effective polysyllables. (The opening word of
the poem, the polysyllabic "Especially", blows a gusty rhythm;
the similarity between "when" and "wind" echoes gently.)

The sound effects in "Especially when the October wind" help
blend harmoniously together the various experiences on an October
day which the poet is attempting to express and simultaneously to
communicate to the reader.

V

"The hand that signed the paper" is characterized by objectivity,
compression, and clarity. It seems particularly important to discuss
some of the artistic devices employed in this poem because very
few of Thomas's poems can be described as objective, compressed,
and clear.

The subjective references common in Thomas's poetry are
lacking in "The hand that signed the paper". Instead, Thomas is
unusually detached from the poem. Throughout the first stanza,
for example, the king is progressively depersonalized and frag-
mented. His "hand" becomes "five sovereign fingers" and finally
— because the fingers that sign the paper symbolize the king's
greatest power — "five kings". In large part the poem's objectivity
is successful because Thomas presents a pitiable situation by stating
only the stark facts — such as "And famine grew, and locusts
came" — and expressing no sentiments. As a result, the reader's
reaction is all the more sincerely sympathetic.

The formal structure of "The hand that signed the paper" is

tightly organized and very functional in that it contributes to the
poem's forcefulness. The four stanzas of four lines each have
the following pattern, which is regular except in the last line of
stanza I:

Stanza	Number of Syllables in Each Line
I	11 8 11 *8*
II	11 8 11 6
III	11 8 11 6
IV	11 8 11 6

The rhythm of the speech stresses in the poem is one of Thomas's
closest approaches to regular iambic. Yet the speech-stress pattern
is not absolutely regular, and the distribution of emphases is related
significantly to the development of the poem. In the first stanza
there are two instances of consecutive stressed syllables ("'Five
'sovereign" and "'These 'five 'kings") and in the second stanza one
instance ("'hand 'leads"). These early occurrences give only a
suggestion of the accumulated emphases of stanza IV; the absence
of such emphases in stanza III makes stanza IV the more forceful.
The final stanza concerns absolute power and rule; it is thus fitting
that the rhythm, reinforcing the meaning, be powerful and emphatic.
The accumulation of consecutive stresses — in "'five 'kings 'count",
"'hand 'rules 'pity", "'hand 'rules 'heaven", and "'no 'tears" —
helps lend the conclusion the desired effect of power and emphasis.

The line-end word arrangement is fairly regular: the first and
third lines of each stanza end in feminine words which (in the unstressed syllable only) rhyme; the second and fourth lines end in
monosyllables which (with the exception of "brow", "flow") are full
rhymes. Supported by generally end-stopped lines, the line-end
words receive considerable emphasis. The position of other important words in the poem seems also to be carefully controlled.
The initial word of each line is either very weak or strong. Half the
lines begin weakly with "A" or "The"; therefore when an important
word begins a line it is further strengthened by contrast with the
initial particles in other lines. For example, witness the effectiveness of the concluding line — "Hands have no tears to flow" —
which follows line 1 beginning with "The", line 2 with "The", and

line 3 with "A". In the medial position in the lines, the high striking power of many of the words gives them forcefulness. This is the more interesting since, in the earlier poems studied, 36 per cent to 55 per cent of the high striking power words occur in initial and terminal positions; in "The hand that signed the paper" only 8 per cent occur in initial or terminal positions, and all the rest in medial positions. The emphases in the terminal position in this poem result from the line-end word arrangement and from the pauses determined by punctuation marks. Only three of the lines have no terminal punctuation, and only one line has internal punctuation. The necessity to pause on a rhyme lends emphasis to the terminal words in the line.

Auditory repetitions within the lines also form a means of increased emphasis. Consider the consonantal echoes in

> The ha*nd* that sig*ned* the paper felle*d* a city
> . . . .
> Dou*B*Le*d* the g*L*o*B*e of dea*d* a*nd* halve*d* a country.

Even more obvious are the syntactical repetitions — e.g., "felled a city", "taxed the breath", "Doubled the globe", "halved a country"; "And famine grew", "and locusts came."

"The hand that signed the paper" is, then, a noteworthy early example of Thomas's correlating sound and sense throughout a poem. The poem concerns power, and the elements of sound enhance emphatic auditory effects.

VI

"Should lanterns shine" is a brief, nineteen-line poem about the youthful narrator's attempts to find a valid guide in life. In structure the poem is looser than any of the poems previously considered, all of which — except "From love's first fever to her plague" — are in regular stanzas of more or less strictly patterned verse. "Should lanterns shine" consists of two long paragraphs followed by two very short paragraphs. The syllabic structure is irregular, with fewer syllables in the lines of the last two paragraphs than in those of the first paragraphs:

Stanza	Number of Syllables in Each Line
I	8 12 10 8 8 10 10 10
II	10 8 10 11 10 14 8
III	9 8
IV	10 6

The line-end words form no pattern, although one instance of rhyme occurs and three instances of initial consonance occur. The metrical stress pattern tends toward iambic tetrameter and iambic pentameter, but the speech stress is diverse.

In its auditory elements as well as in its prosodic structure the poem shows less obvious patterning than most of Thomas's earlier pieces. Further, the tempo of the first two paragraphs is somewhat faster than that of the last two paragraphs. In the opening ones, the comparatively long poetic statements, the several polysyllables, and the predominance of vowel sounds over consonantal sounds tend to produce a swift rhythm. A main auditory element of the opening paragraphs, for example, is the rather high frequency of a vowel sound as the initial or final syllable of a word, as in

> Caught *in* *a*n *o*ctagon *of* *u*naccustomed light
>
> . . . .
>
> The mumm*y* clothes *e*xpose *a*n *a*ncient breast
>
> . . . .
>
> *A*nd, when *it* quickens, *a*lter th*e* *a*ctions pace.

The emphasis in the poem upon vowel sounds and the sparseness of consonantal clusters make particularly prominent any repetition of consonants; witness the use in

> Ti*ll* fie*l*d and roof *l*ie *l*eve*l* and the same.

The prolonged effect of the continuant *l* — especially since it is repeated five times within a single line — makes the rhythm smoothly reinforce the meaning.

In sound and sense "Should lanterns shine" provides a contrast between the diversity of the first two paragraphs and the succinctness of the last two. In the first two paragraphs of the poem, the narrator considers various guides in life. But he believes that conventional religions are satisfactory guides only when one accepts unquestioningly the basic assumptions; i.e., religions are valid only "in their private dark". The rituals (clothes) of conventional religions are, he thinks, outdated, ancient, mummied. Other guides are equally faulty. Both the heart and the mind are helpless guides, the narrator feels, and instinct is an unreliable guide. In the final two paragraphs he muses upon the fact that for years he has been trying the suggested guides, "And many years should see some change". But his years' long search for a valid guide is still incomplete:

> The ball I threw while playing in the park
> Has not yet reached the ground.

These cryptic, symbolic final two lines climax the poem and are distinctive in large part because of the contrast with the earlier paragraphs. The longer lines and paragraphs of the opening, its swifter tempo and its unobtrusive patterning set apart and emphasize the poem's succinct conclusion.

VII

"And death shall have no dominion", one of Thomas's best-known poems, concerns immortality viewed from spiritual and physical focuses. As Thomas E. Connolly has observed, stanza I depicts heaven, stanza II depicts hell, and stanza III treats of the physical indestructibility of man.[15]

Each of the three stanzas is of nine lines, but the pattern of the syllabic verse is irregular:

Stanza	Number of Syllables in Each Line
I	8 8 10 11 9 8 11 8 8
II	8 8 10 9 9 8 10 7 8
III	8 8 8 11 9 8 11 9 8

Speech stresses vary considerably. Over half the lines open with a

[15] See "Thomas' 'And Death Shall Have No Dominion'", *Explicator*, XIV (January, 1956), item 33.

stressed syllable, and many lines contain both anapests and iambs. Occasional consecutive stressed syllables stand out clearly and underscore heavily the meaning of the word, as in the staccato phrases "'Dead 'men 'naked", "'clean 'bones 'gone", and "'split 'all 'ends 'up". Unpatterned, too, is the use of assonance and final consonance in the terminal words of the lines. Yet, not only do most of the line-end words end in a punctuated pause, but they also end in an *n* sound. Thereby the thematically important word "dominion" is emphasized. The poem is linked structurally, however, less by patterns of stresses, of line-end words, and of pauses than by syntactical repetitions. For example, consecutive lines in stanza I begin respectively with "They", "Though they", "Though they", "Though", and the first and last lines of each stanza repeat the theme-statement, "And death shall have no dominion".

In certain lines the vowel and consonantal arrangements complement the meaning. Two of the key words in the line "And death shall have no dominion" are related by alliteration of the sound *d*: "death" and "dominion". The short vowel *æ* occurs in three unstressed words ("And", "shall", "have"). The only other word in the line ("no") has its consonant echoed twice in the succeeding word, "dominion". The assonance and consonance in the statement of the theme do, then, help it to ring with conviction. Other lines also have interesting auditory affinities. One line from each stanza will be selected for comment.

In stanza I the transposition of the well-known phrases "the man in the moon" and "the west wind" into

With the man in the wind and the west moon

creates an intricate, melodious auditory pattern. "Wind" and "west" are linked by alliteration, and "wind" is further related to three unstressed words, to "with" by alliteration and assonance, to "in" by assonance, and to "and" by final consonance. "Man" and "moon" are linked by both initial and final consonance. Moreover, the graphs of the striking power and vowel tone for this line are closely parallel.

Stanza I, line 3

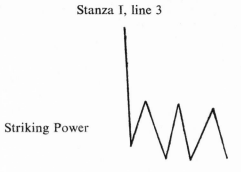

Striking Power

Vowel Tone

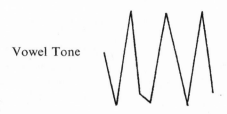

In stanza II in the line "Twisting on racks when sinews give way", all the stressed vowels are short and high (reflecting the fitfulness and intensity of the pain of the damned) till the swift tempo and increasing pressure are relieved by the long *e* sound (reflecting the contrast in meaning here, the physical giving way of the tortured sinews). There is a marked contrast also between the consonants at the beginning and the end of the line. The unvoiced sibilants and explosives of the beginning give the impression of abruptness and effort, and the semivowel of "way" gives the impression of soft continuity and auditory "giving way". Yet, as the later lines signify, those in hell never die; they live in eternal punishment. In stanza III the theme is expressed by the image of vegetable life renewing itself and popping up:

Heads of the characters hammer through daisies.

The line is quite rapid, because no heavy syllables slow down the rhythm. The strong, pulsating dactylic meter further suggests the meaning of the entire poem — the corollary of "death shall have no dominion" — life is triumphant.

VIII

"It is the sinners' dust-tongued bell", one of Thomas's so-called marriage poems, is in five stanzas of six lines each. The syllabic pattern, however, is quite irregular, although lines 3 and 6 are always shorter and have fewer stresses than the other lines.

Stanza	Number of Syllables in Each Line					
I	13	12	8	13	12	8
II	11	14	8	13	12	8
III	13	12	8	13	15	8
IV	14	13	7	13	15	7
V	15	14	8	15	14	8

The speech stresses are also irregular, except that lines 3 and 6 usually have fewer stresses than the other lines. The metrical pattern varies, often to suit the meaning of the individual line. Note the variety of meter and meaning in the following lines. On the one hand, the sets of consecutive stressed monosyllables in "'Time 'marks a 'black 'aisle" stalks slowly, reinforcing the meaning. On the other hand, the two anapests separated by an iamb in "In a 'holy 'room in a 'wave" flow smoothly and — supported by the unobtrusive continuants and semivowel — very quietly.

But what gives the stanzas their specific organization is the pattern of final consonance in the line-end words. This consonance links lines 1 and 4, 2 and 5, 3 and 6, so that the pattern is *abcabc*. The only variations in the scheme are in pairing the *ks* sound of "fireworks" with the *k* sound of "weather-cock", the voiceless *s* sound of "house" with the voiced *z* sound of "prays", and the voiced *v* sound of "wave" with the voiceless *f* sound of "grief".

Not only the vertical patterning of consonance in the terminal syllables of lines, but also the horizontal patterning of vowels and consonants make "It is the sinners' dust-tongued bell" interesting in the study of Thomas's development of auditory techniques. In one line, for instance, explosives predominate:

Hear *by d*eath's acci*dent* the *c*loc*ked* an*d d*ashe*d-d*own s*p*ires.

The poet accentuates the harsh, sharp effect of these thirteen explosives by introducing the line with the imperative "Hear". The slow tempo of the phrase "and dashed-down" stems in part from the device of juxtaposing, at the end of one word and the beginning of the next word, the same sound. The sheer physical necessity to pause and repeat the explosive *d* retards the tempo of the end of the line.[16] Through such techniques Thomas helps sound reinforce sense, in this case the harsh, insistent striking of the spire's clock.

In contrast to his use of sharp explosives is his use of voiced continuants to produce a sensation of calm. The phrase "the emerald, still bell" is an illustration. Each of the three occurrences of the *l* sound seems more sustained than the preceding one. The melodic effect is also evident from the analysis of the patterns of striking power and vowel tone, which are essentially parallel:

Stanza III, line 5, syllables iii-vii

Striking Power

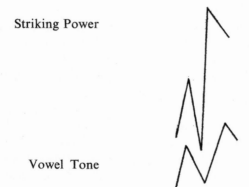

Vowel Tone

"It is the sinners' dust-tongued bell", like "And death shall have no dominion", demonstrates, in selected and individual lines, a variety of sounds and meanings: staccato rhythms and compressed meanings, and — less frequently — more sustained rhythms and simpler meaning.

[16]   All the other occurrences of the phenomenon in the poem are similar in retarding the rhythm and reinforcing the meaning of the words: "dust-tongued", "Time marks", "mute turrets", and (except for the difference between the unvoiced and voiced quality) "love's sinners".

IX

"After the Funeral" ("In Memory of Ann Jones") is, according to Thomas, the only poem he wrote directly about the life and death of a particular person he knew.[17] Thomas composed the poem in February, 1933, in a short form consisting of the first fifteen lines, ending with: "Round the parched worlds of Wales and drowned each sun." He later criticized this original version as "feeble"; in particular he felt the ending was "too facile &, almost, grandiosely sentimental".[18] In March, 1938, he revised and greatly lengthened the poem. Even after carefully reworking the poem, Thomas felt dissatisfied with it in certain respects. To Vernon Watkins he wrote: "I think there are some good lines, but don't know abt the thing as a whole."[19] And Theodore Roethke remembers that Thomas thought the opening lines "creaked a bit" and believed he had not worked hard enough on them.[20]

Despite Thomas's doubts, "After the Funeral" is a brilliant — though somewhat uncharacteristic — poem. It is an elegy for a little-known but devout and "ancient peasant"[21] woman whose death meant desolation to the young boy from whose point of view the poem is written. The poem is one long paragraph of forty lines, each with ten, eleven, or twelve syllables of which four, five, or six receive speech stresses. The line-end words reveal no definite scheme, but occasional initial sound similarities occur (as in "sleeves", "sleep", "leaves") and frequent final consonantal similarities occur (as in "thick", "black"; "fern", "alone", "Ann"; "virtue", "statue"; "window", "hollow", to present only a few). Because of

---

[17] See *Quite Early one Morning* (Norfolk, Conn., 1954), p. 174. Rayner Heppenstall says — in *The Four Absentees* (London, 1960), pp. 174-175 — that he substituted for Thomas in a lecture at Oxford when Thomas gave the excuse that an aunt had died. Heppenstall suggests that perhaps the funeral was that of Ann Jones. If, however, the lecture date is 1949, the hypothesis is implausible, for the poem on Ann Jones was written in 1933 and revised in 1938.

[18] *LVW*, p. 57.

[19] *Ibid.*, p. 58.

[20] "Dylan Thomas: Memories and Appreciations", *Encounter*, II (January, 1954), p. 11.

[21] *LVW*, p. 58.

the nature of the line-end words and because most of the lines are run-on, the lines flow relatively freely from one to another.

Thomas's original fifteen-line version, the first of the two main sections of the poem, is a description of Ann's burial. The opening lines reflect the insincerity of the mourners' tributes, tears, and hand-shaking: "mule praises, brays, / Windshake of sailshaped ears ...." The proximity of the near-rhyme in "praises, brays" — note the startling contrast in meaning — and of the alliteration and assonance in "Windshake of sailshaped" helps create the desired effect of the monotony of hypocritical funeral-formalities. The muffled pegging down of the coffin is aptly described by the phrase "muffled-toed tap / Tap happily", with its strong rhythm and its alliteration, repetition, and rhyme. When these hollow, slightly comical sights and sounds culminate in the final funeral ceremony of shoveling dirt over the coffin ("smack[ing] ... the spade that wakes up sleep"), the boy suddenly realizes his great loss. Alone in Ann's room with its stuffed fox and stale fern, he recalls Ann's humility and goodness. In his loneliness he remembers her overflowing love, her

> ... hooded, fountain heart [which] once fell in puddles
> Round the parched worlds of Wales and drowned each sun.

In parenthetical thoughts the narrator discharges himself of any sentimentality in his tribute to Ann's infinite love, by criticizing her love as "a monstrous image blindly / Magnified out of praise", which Ann would have considered pretentious and unnecessary.

Although Ann needs no priest of praise ("no druid"), the narrator says he must sing of her virtues to diminish his own grief. And lines 21-40 form the second portion of the poem, the boy's homage to the deceased. Sound echoes become more frequent and obvious in this part of the poem. For example, internal rhyme is closely juxtaposed in "call all", "sing and swing", and "breast and blessed". The poem becomes a hymnic crescendo — and a "sculptured" one because many of the consonantal clusters produce abrupt, staccato effects. The narrator demands that Ann's natural virtues be recognized in the hymning heads, the woods, and the chapel and that her spirit be blessed by a symbolic "four, crossing birds". Again the narrator mentions Ann's meekness and excuses his praise (i.e.,

his "skyward statue") of her on the ground that otherwise his grief
would be insufferable. But his final efforts to depict her realistically
only sculpture her virtues:

> I know her scrubbed and sour humble hands
> Lie with religion in their cramp, her threadbare
> Whisper in a damp word, her wits drilled hollow,
> Her fist of a face died clenched on a round pain.

These four lines — perhaps the best in the poem — reveal that such
devices as assonance ("scrubbed", "humble"), alliteration ("humble
hands"), and occasional rhyme ("cramp" "damp") are relatively
obvious and that the contrapuntal imagery in the poem, which
refers to Ann as the actual peasant woman and as the monumental
figure the narrator envisions her,[22] is relatively subtle. In the
brilliant but uncharacteristic "After the Funeral" Thomas has not
yet fused sound and sense as he does in later poems.

X

"When all my five and country senses see" is a quasi-sonnet with
ten-plus-four lines but without a prescribed rhyme scheme. Some
full rhyme does exist (in "eye", "by", "cry" and in "awake",
"break"), but more often the relationship between line-end words
is less well-defined (for instance, the final consonance in "mark",
"zodiac"). Yet, with two exceptions, the poem has ten syllables in
each line and, sonnet-like, its metrical pattern is iambic pentameter.

In the first ten lines, the poet presents his argument that certain
sensations belonging to one sense or mode attach to certain sensations of another sense or mode. When all the five natural ("country")
senses see, he says, they will become cross-modal and see the des-
truction of their province of love. Thus the fingers will forget their
role in love and fertility and see how love is subservient to time
and death; the ears will see how love is drummed away in discord;
the tongue will see and lament that the "fond wounds" of love are
mended; the nostrils will see that the breath of love burns and is
consumed by its own fire. In the last four lines the poet presents an

---

[22] See C. Day-Lewis's *The Poetic Image*, pp. 125-127, for a discussion of the
contrapuntal imagery in "After the Funeral".

emphatic conclusion. The heart, he believes, has agents in all the provinces of love. These are emotional energies which will become effective ("grope awake") when the five senses sleep or perish. The heart, then, is sensual and knowing; even when all else fails, it can rekindle man's responsiveness to the world about him.

A basic aspect of Thomas's thought seems revealed in this poem. The five senses, Thomas believes, are elements that contribute to the sovereign part of man — "my one and noble heart", the repository of feeling and knowledge. On this axiom Thomas's poetic theory seems to be based, for sound and sense in his poetry are both usually employed to elicit from the reader an emotional — as opposed to an intellectual — response. It is significant, perhaps, that this poem which postulates Thomas's fundamental concept of the importance of the sensual heart contains few of Thomas's usual devices for auditory correlation. The lack of internal arrangements of vowel and consonant sounds, for example, is noteworthy. Probably Thomas realized that, since he was writing directly about the senses, it would be more effective not to appeal to the senses through elaborate auditory links.

CHAPTER II

Thomas's second poetic period extends from 1939 to 1945, the years of World War II. The year 1939 was important to Thomas not only for the outbreak of the war, but also for the birth, on January 30, of Llewelyn, his first child. These two events seem to have influenced significantly Thomas's poetic approach, for both caused him to look beyond himself. As a result, Thomas's poetry of the war years is less subjective and more concerned with others than is his earlier verse. This concern for others is expressed in three poems written at the close of his first poetic period: "I make this in a warring absence", a poem, written in November, 1937, to his wife, Caitlin; "After the Funeral", a poem, revised in March, 1938, about a dead aunt; "A saint about to fall", a poem, written in October, 1938, about Thomas's unborn son, Llewelyn. Between 1939 and 1945 Thomas wrote poems about his son ("This Side of Truth — for Llewelyn") and about victims of air raids ("Among those killed in the Dawn Raid was a Man Aged a Hundred", "Ceremony After a Fire Raid", and "A Refusal to Mourn the Death, by Fire, of a Child in London").

Even the war work in which Thomas participated had beneficial influences upon his poetry. As a script writer for the British Broadcasting Company, Thomas developed a sense of unity and of theme, which he applied to his poetry. Unlike the "obscure" poetry of his first poetic period, most of the later poetry of his second period is sustained by a unifying mood or idea. Much of it is grave and formal ceremonial or hymnic poetry, such as "There was a Saviour", "On the Marriage of a Virgin", "Ceremony After a Fire Raid", "A Refusal to Mourn the Death, by Fire, of a Child in London."

His war work influenced not only the theme, but also the rhythm of the poetry. As a close observation of Thomas's prose — especially "A Child's Christmas in Wales" — will indicate conclusively, his prose and poetry rhythms are essentially similar. Stephen Spender wrote in 1946, after listening to Thomas read on the radio his childhood memories of Christmas, "I understood at once the patterns of his recent poetry, which are essentially patterns of speech, the music of rhetoric."[1]

Thomas's second poetic period is fundamentally, then, one of poetic transition. The early poems of the period (e.g., "'If my head hurt a hair's foot'") are similar to those of the first poetic period; the very late poems of the period ("Poem in October", "Fern Hill", and "In my Craft or Sullen Art") are similar to those of the third poetic period. Yet the second period does have general characteristics of its own. Primarily, it reveals the development toward a more expansive, open-work poetry, and it reveals part of the basis for this development, the influence upon Thomas of his work during World War II and of the birth of his first child.

The twelve poems analyzed in the following commentaries are representative of the variety of poetry in Thomas's second, transitional period:

     XI – "'If my head hurt a hair's foot'"
    XII – "Once below a time"
   XIII – "There was a Saviour"
   XIV – "On the Marriage of a Virgin"
    XV – "The Ballad of the Long-legged Bait"
   XVI – "The Hunchback in the Park"
  XVII – "Ceremony After a Fire Raid"
 XVIII – "Poem in October"
   XIX – "A Refusal to Mourn the Death, by Fire,
               of a Child in London"
    XX – "A Winter's Tale"
   XXI – "Fern Hill"
  XXII – "In my Craft or Sullen Art"

[1] "Poetry for Poetry's Sake and Poetry Beyond Poetry", *Horizon*, XIII (April, 1946), p. 234.

XI

"'If my head hurt a hair's foot'" is a dialogue between an unborn child, who speaks in the first three stanzas, and its mother, who speaks in the last three stanzas. The form of the poem is stanzaic, with five lines in each of the six stanzas. The syllabic, metrical, and speech-stress patterns are irregular. However, in the first three stanzas the lines are generally shorter and yet usually have more speech stresses than in the last three stanzas. In respect to line-end word arrangement, the first three stanzas contain only scattered assonance and final consonance, but the last three stanzas contain instances of full rhyme ("bed", "head" and "cave", "grave") and a concentration, in stanza VI, of final consonance ("grain", "return", "stone", "open").

With its arbitrary, verbal conceits and its obvious consonantal patterns, the first part of "'If my head hurt a hair's foot'" is reminiscent of Thomas's style in many of the poems of his early period. The opening lines, for instance, have multiple occurrences of the similar-sounding labial stops *b* and *p*:

> "If my head hurt a hair's foot
> Pack back the downed bone. If the unpricked ball of my breath
> Bump on a spout let the bubbles jump out."

The bouncing alliterative *b*'s in "back", "bone", "ball", "breath", "bump", "bubbles" are in initial positions. The *p*'s in "unpricked", "bump", "spout", "jump" are in internal or final positions. Combined with this cacophony of consonantal arrangement are the closely juxtaposed internal rhymes in "Pack", "back"; "Bump", "jump"; "spout", "out"; and the approximate rhyme in "downed", "bone". To make the rhythm even more abrupt, almost every word in these lines is a monosyllable. The harsh staccato effect seems, then, to be carefully worked out. But whether or not such an effect is *appropriate* here is another matter. It is important to distinguish between sound patterns and poetic values and not, as Henry Treece does, simply to dismiss these opening lines as a "humourless plethora of sound and deafness."[2] Even Thomas was

---

[2]   *Dylan Thomas: 'Dog Among the Fairies'* (London, 1957), p. 89.

aware of an unresolved problem in the lines; he wrote to Vernon Watkins, "I haven't been able to alter the first part, & will have to leave it unsuccessful."[3]

In the third stanza, the child in the womb makes a more effective plea to his mother than in the introductory lines. He makes the startling suggestion that

> "If my bunched, monkey coming is cruel
> Rage me back to the making house...."

Here sound correlates with sense. For example, the repetition of the explosive k sound ("monkey coming is cruel", "back", "making") and the repetition of the Λ vowel followed by the nasal m or n (in "bunched monkey coming") creates a pronounced and insistent rhythm which reinforces the implied situation of the new mother in labor.

In the second section of the poem, the mother expresses her awareness that the anguish she and her child must experience in life is inescapable and comments that once life begins, suffering must be endured. In contrast to the child's staccato speech, the mother's speech is relatively flowing. Whereas the child often uses consecutively stressed monosyllables with short vowels, such as "Peck", "sprint", "dance", the mother uses few accumulations of stresses and thus creates a looser rhythm; whereas the child uses compressed, obvious consonantal arrangements, the mother uses expanded, echoic consonantal arrangements. Among the most subtle auditory links in the second section of the poem is the repetition, in stanza V, of the same long vowel or diphthong in a stressed position both near the beginning and near the end of a line:

"Now to awake husked of gestures and my joy like a cave

. . . .

O my lost love bounced from a good home;
The grain that hurries this way from the rim of the grave
Has a voice and a house, and there and here you must couch and cry."

This artistic device is echoed and intensified in the final stanza,

[3] *LVW*, p. 60.

where the words are linked not simply by assonance, but (as in "grain" and "grave" in stanza V) by approximate rhyme: "'Through the waves of the fat streets nor the skeleton's thin ways.'"

The stylistic contrast between the two sections of the poem — the more staccato first section and the more legato second section — helps to set in relief the attitudes of the child and mother toward life. In the final analysis, that attitude is, as Thomas phrased it, the "unreconciled acceptance of suffering".[4] This idea Thomas attempted to indicate in the final line, which he originally wrote as

> And the endless tremendous beginning suffers open.

He felt deep concern for this line — "Is the last line too bad, too comic, or does it *just* work?" — and asked Vernon Watkins for criticism, especially of the adjective.[5] A few weeks later Thomas had, apparently to his satisfaction, reworked the line to

> And the endless beginning of prodigies suffers open.

Thomas's revision is illuminating. Although only the central portion of the line was altered, the effect is considerably changed. In the original version, internal rhyming of syllables ("end-" and "-mend-", "tre-" and "be-") weakens the line with a slightly sing-song effect.[6] In the final version the word "tremendous" (which is responsible for the internal rhymes and, in addition, is an overworked word in the English vocabulary) has been deleted. Although the new line has only one more syllable than the original, the meter is now a strong, almost regular anapest. The new word, "prodigies", deepens the meaning of the entire poem, for its associations with wonders and marvels conclude the poem on a note of awe, if not of hope.

---

[4] *Quite Early One Morning* (Norfolk, Conn., 1954), p. 129.
[5] *LVW*, p. 58.
[6] That Thomas was acutely conscious of such weak internal rhymes is illustrated in a letter to Vernon Watkins in which Thomas chooses "formed" instead of "made" (in the following lines from "There was a Saviour") to avoid "the too-pretty internal rhyme of 'laid' & 'made' [which] ... stops the too-easy flow, or thin conceited stream":
> And laid your cheek against a cloud-formed shell.
(*LVW*, p. 83.)

XII

"Once below a time" describes the poet's attitude toward the human situation, with particular reference to his poetic career. As a poet past his prime (i.e., "now shown and mostly bare"), the *persona* reflects on his pre-natal existence, childhood, and early creative life.

Part I consists of two paragraphs, one of twelve lines, the other of sixteen lines. The number of syllables in the lines varies, in no regular pattern, from five to twelve. The first paragraph describes the poet in his pre-natal existence of

> ... pinned-around-the-spirit
> Cut-to-measure flesh bit,
> Suit for a serial sum.

The short lines, short vowels, clipped explosives, and predominant trochaic meter create an effect of the staccato, pulsating tempo of new life. The line-end word arrangements reinforce this impression, for most of the related line-end words of the first paragraph end in final consonance of explosives: "spiri*t*", "*bit*", "jacke*t*", "ash*pit*".

The second paragraph, continuing the *tour de force* style, celebrates the poet's birth. The poet sees his early self as violent and somewhat arrogant and deceitful. From the beginning, the poet says, he adopted lavish disguises, even though he was actually robed in "common clay clothes". (The harsh alliterative *k's* stick together as clay itself does.) In this paragraph the proximity of diverse auditory effects suggests the protean aspects of childhood. For example, "*Hopp*ing *hot* leave*d*", with its initial consonance of a spirant, its assonance, and its use of explosives (*p, t, d*), creates a clipped rhythm; sound and sense here suggest the child in action. Two lines later, "the chill, silent centre", with its repetition of the continuant *l*, its alliteration of the sibilant *s*, and its approximate rhyme in "si*lent cent*re", creates the impression of stillness; sound and sense here suggest the child in quiet thought. As an imaginative and ambitious child, the boy "rocketed to astonish" not just Wales, but the world itself with his exciting, unrestrained poetic language.

Part II consists of three paragraphs with, respectively, six, six, and eleven lines. The line-end word arrangement is irregular, but does contain several instances of full rhyme: "rotten", "cotton" (which are close together, but in different paragraphs and help link together the first two paragraphs); "head", "thread", "bed"; "stone", "bone", and the near-rhyme "down". In this section the poem is less flamboyant and more sustained and bardic in tone. The mature poet sees his early scales and mask pierced through to reveal

> ... the boy of common thread,
> The bright pretender, the ridiculous sea dandy

who, like all mortals, is simply "dry flesh and earth". Now, although the poet criticizes his immature self, he feels nostalgic toward the lost innocence of childhood when he felt firmly convinced of the triumph of his poetry, when he felt he "Never never oh never [would] ... regret the bugle [he] ... wore". Abruptly, the tone shifts, and the final three lines are markedly calm. Thomas here reveals the *persona* from whom the poem has been written. The mature poet is resigned, humbled, and saddened:

> Now shown and mostly bare I would lie down,
> Lie down, lie down and live
> As quiet as a bone.

Originally the poet's childhood attitude was expressed by the line "I do not regret the bugle I wore". Thomas revised the line to

> Never never oh never to regret the bugle I wore,

so that "the repetition, the pacific repetition, of 'I would lie down, lie down, lie down and live' is loudly and swingingly balanced".[7]

In the last three lines, the extensive use of voiced continuants (e.g., the *n* of "*N*ow, show*n*", "dow*n*", "bo*n*e" and the *l* of "most*l*y", "*l*ie", and "*l*ive") and the repetition of long vowels (e.g., the *o* of "sh*o*wn", "m*o*stly", "b*o*ne" and the *ai* of "*I*", "l*ie*", "qu*ie*t") contribute to the lyrical effect of the concluding passage. This lyricism differs sharply from the staccato effects of many of the earlier portions of the poem; thus the contrast in sound patterns reinforces

---

[7]   *LVW*, pp. 79-80.

the contrast in meaning between the attitude of the immature and of the mature poet. Thomas's reading of this poem, on tape at the University of Florida, further points up this contrast between the optimism of childhood and the resignation of later life, for he reads most of the poem loudly and energetically, but these final lines, very quietly and evenly till the word "bone" resounds hollowly.

XIII

Although Thomas usually experiments with an original stanzaic pattern (and seldom uses that pattern twice), "There was a Saviour" is a lyrical poem based on the stanza of Milton's "On the Morning of Christ's Nativity".[8] But Thomas's stanzaic form is considerably shorter and looser than Milton's. "On the Morning of Christ's Nativity" contains a four-stanza Invocation — with seven lines to a stanza and the rhyme scheme of *ababbcc* — which has no equivalent in "There was a Saviour". It is "The Hymn", the body of the poem, on which Thomas patterned his piece. Milton's twenty-seven stanzas contain eight lines each and use a syllabic pattern — sometimes slightly varied — of 6 6 10 6 6 10 8 12. Thomas's pattern in "There was a Saviour" is quite similar:

Stanza	Number of Syllables in Each Line
I	6 6 11 6 6 10 9 11
II	6 6 11 6 6 10 10 12
III	6 7 11 6 8 11 10 13
IV	6 6 10 6 6 10 10 12
V	6 6 10 6 6 10 9 12

In respect to line-end rhyme, Milton's scheme is *aabccbdd*. Thomas uses the same scheme, but instead of full rhyme he employs assonance in the final syllables. With two exceptions ("Saviour",

---

[8] In writing to Vernon Watkins, Thomas referred to "There was a Saviour" as his "austere poem in Milton measure". (*LVW*, p. 82.) It is perhaps noteworthy that Kathleen Raine says she has been told that Milton's "Nativity Ode" was Thomas's favorite poem. ("Dylan Thomas", *New Statesman and Nation*, XLVI [November 14, 1953], p. 594.)

"radium" and "year", "neighbor") the assonance is perfectly
regular throughout the poem.

Certainly Thomas's and Milton's poems bear little resemblance
other than in general stanzaic form. The setting for the "Nativity
Ode" is the "happy morn" of Christ's birth, and the mood is deeply
reverent; the setting for "There was a Saviour" is the present age
of science, doubt, and sin, and the emphasis in the poem is on
"There *was* a Saviour".

Throughout his poetry Thomas frequently employs striking
introductory phrases. Sometimes these revolve around a paradox,
such as "Friend by enemy I call you out" and "Light breaks where
no sun shines", or a revitalized familiar phrase, such as "A grief
ago" and "Once below a time". None is, however, more arresting
or utilizes more appropriate artistic devices than

> There was a Saviour
> Rarer than radium
> Commoner than water, crueller than truth,

which is a network of alliteration and assonance. The *r* sound is
found in most of the important words of the passage. In the third
line, the *k* sound lends emphasis to the words "Commoner" and
"crueller". Such euphony of consonants is complemented by the
euphony of vowels. The line-end word relationship between
"Saviour" and "radium" is particularly interesting because it is a
tri-syllabic near-rhyme. This, in addition to the internal rhyme in
"There", "rarer", strongly intensifies the echo effect. That Thomas
was conscious of subtle internal patterns of sound in this poem is
evident from his comment on the internal pattern of consonance
in stanza I, lines 1 and 2. Of the passage

> Two proud, blacked brothers cry,
> Winter-locked side by side,

he said: "I like the word 'blacked' ... in spite of its, in the context,
jarring dissonance with 'locked'."[9]

"There was a Saviour", in its looser stanzaic form, more subtle
artistic devices, and relatively lyrical mood approaches Thomas's
style in his third poetic period. It is the meaning in this poem

⁹ *LVW*, p. 82.

which, in its general compression, links "There was a Saviour" with the poetry of Thomas's early period. The poet seems to say that Christ is available to men of true humility but that most of us crucified Christ and now cry in the dark of self-pity

> ... for the little known fall,
> For the dropping of homes
>   That did not nurse our bones
> Brave deaths of only ones but never found.

Concluding hopefully, the poet suggests that, through the terrible realization of our sins, we may see

> Exiled in us ... the soft,
> Unclenched, armless, silk and rough love that breaks all rocks.

XIV

"On the Marriage of a Virgin" is a fourteen-line poem originally written in 1933, but revised and first published in 1941. Interpretations of the poem vary. David Daiches and Derek Stanford believe the poem contrasts the state of virginity with the state of marriage; S. F. Johnson believes it contrasts human and supernatural love; Bernard Kneiger believes it describes the poetic conception of the birth of Christ. Whatever the specific meaning, the theme of the poem — like that of many of Thomas's prose tales — concerns something which can never again be recaptured and implies a contrast between the past and the present. It is not impossible that in this poem Thomas intended that the exact nature of the contrast be ambiguous and thus generalized.

Throughout, the poem is stately in rhythm, resonant in tone, and solemn in mood. In part, the majestic but melancholy quality stems from the use of the long vowel o, which occurs in 16 per cent of the speech-stressed syllables: "alone", "morning", "opening", "golden", "old", "loaves", "moment", "alone", "golden ghost", "bone", "golden", and "coursing". The frequency of this vowel is particularly impressive since, according to Godfrey Dewey, the o vowel in normal speech represents only 1.6 per cent of the vowels and consonants.

Two other vowels in "On the Marriage of a Virgin" each
form 15 per cent of the speech-stressed syllables: *ai* and ʌ.
Three vowels, then, form nearly half the vowels in the speech-
stressed syllables. Because of the predominance of the vowel
sounds, the avoidance of harsh consonantal clusters, and the use
of voiced continuants (primarily *l*, *m*, *r*), the rhythm is flowing and
sustained. The even cadence is, significantly, seldom interrupted
by words of high striking power; of all the poems under consideration, "On the Marriage of a Virgin" has proportionately the
fewest words of high striking power (one out of every eighteen
words).

Although the poem has fourteen lines, it has little else of prosodic
structure in common with a conventional sonnet. The organization
is achieved by two seven-line stanzas; the syllabic pattern is somewhat irregular:

Stanza	Number of Syllables in Each Line
I	15 12 13 12 16 15 16
II	14 12 13 15 16 14 15

and the metrical pattern is varied. Further, the poem lacks a rhyme
pattern characteristic of the sonnet. In fact, the only full rhyme
occurs in lines 2 and 4 of each stanza: "eyes", "thighs"; "alone",
"bone". The other line-end words are linked, in no regular scheme,
mainly by assonance or by final consonance.

"On the Marriage of a Virgin" is one of Thomas's first poems
entirely in a sustained legato rhythm. The serious treatment of the
theme, the provocative imagery, and the stately rhythm (influenced
mainly by careful combinations of low or middle vowels with voiced
continuants) make the poem consistently majestic and solemn in
both sound and sense.

XV

In respect to its poetic value, probably the most controversial of
Thomas's poems is his longest one, "The Ballad of the Long-legged
Bait". On the one hand, Henry Treece condemns its length, fifty-
four stanzas of four lines each, as "tiring" and its total effect as

"little more than a technical exercise".[10] On the other hand, Elder Olson considers the poem one of Thomas's best.[11] The true evaluation of the poem almost certainly lies between these extremes. But it is undeniable that the poem contains characteristics of Thomas's best and most visionary poems.

Of all Thomas's works, "The Ballad of the Long-legged Bait" is most enhanced by Thomas's reading of it. The reader of the printed page bogs down in the long and complicated allegory; the listener to Thomas's reading soars into a new world of words. Because "The Ballad of the Long-legged Bait" is a poem of music with an intensely personal vision, the sound and emotional contexts of the words are usually effective only when the poem is heard. In describing this poem, Thomas might have echoed Hamlet, "The word's the thing". It *is* a fact that he told Alastair Reid that "When I experience anything, I experience it as a thing and a word at the same time, both equally amazing".[12] With respect to "The Ballad of the Long-legged Bait", Thomas was especially conscious of words: he said the writing of the poem was "like carrying a huge armful of words to a table he thought was upstairs and wondering if he could reach it in time, or if it would still be there".[13]

The structure of "The Ballad of the Long-legged Bait" is a loose ballad stanza. The poem always has four lines to a stanza, but the stresses are not often in the regular ballad meter of *4 3 4 3*. Further, the typical ballad handles casually an *abcb* rhyme scheme, but in Thomas's poem the line-end word relationships vary and the pattern of relationship is also flexible. Only in one-third of the stanzas is the pattern of relationship *abcb*. In about 40 per cent of the stanzas the pattern is *abab*; in about 28 per cent of the stanzas other patterns occur. The type of line-end word relationship runs the gamut from no similar sounds to eye rhyme and full rhyme. No similarity in sound occurs in 20 per cent of the paired line-end words; some degree of final consonance appears in over 50 per cent; full rhyme

[10] *Dylan Thomas: 'Dog Among the Fairies'*, p. 97.
[11] See *The Poetry of Dylan Thomas* (Chicago, 1954), p. 24.
[12] "A First Word", *Yale Literary Magazine*, CXXII (November, 1954). Reprinted in John Malcolm Brinnin, *A Casebook on Dylan Thomas* (New York, 1960), p. 255.
[13] *Idem*.

occurs in about 15 per cent; other line-end word relationships occur in about 15 per cent. The progression in the poem is from an accumulation of more obvious relationships — for instance, in the first third of the poem half the full rhymes occur — to less obvious and more complex echoes. Such a progression in the sound structure is fitting for a poem whose meaning glides from an apparently simple ballad style to an increasingly complex allegorical style.

Analysis reveals that the rich, seemingly spontaneous overflow of evocative and musically haunting words in the poem results largely from numerous and involved internal vowel and consonant patterns. Although these patterns permeate "The Ballad of the Long-legged Bait", they seem concentrated in the passages of greatest importance to the meaning of the allegory. The following discussion will attempt to relate the sound and sense of several of these passages.

With a hooked bride as bait, a fisherman sails away from the land. Thinking that he is escaping the monotonous common-placeness of life, he is oblivious even to religious portents and is concerned only with his adventure in sexuality:

> Good-bye to chimneys and funnels,
> Old wives that spin in the smoke
> He was blind to the eyes of candles
> In the praying windows of waves
> But heard his bait buck in the wake
> And tussle in a shoal of loves.

The first four lines contain vertical echoes ("chim-", "spin in", and "win-"), assonance ("-bye", "wives", "blind", "eyes"; and "pray-" "waves"), and approximate rhyme ("wives", "waves"). The flowing rhythm contrasts sharply with the bucking rhythm of the opening line of the succeeding stanza. Several elements contribute to the clipped, jerky effect of this line: the series of eight short mono-syllables, the presence of numerous explosives (b, t, d, and k), and the patterned interlocking of the dominant consonants and vowels. The line "And tussle in a shoal of loves", with its prominent con-tinuants (s and l), provides a marked contrast to the previous line.

It contains only one explosive (the *t*, which occurs early in the line), and its unvoiced sounds disappear toward the end. Thus the sounds of these lines gradually soften, till the conclusion itself is quite fluid.

After the fisherman has cast his long-legged bait as a symbolic sacrifice to a watery grave, the sympathetic creatures of the world

> Sing and howl through sand and anemone
> Valley and sahara in a shell,
> Oh all the wanting flesh his enemy
> Thrown to the sea in the shell of a girl.

The ringing quality of the lines can be attributed to such phenomena as the voiced consonants (*l*, *m*, *n*, *r*), the alliteration of the *s* sound ("sing", "sand", "sahara", and "sea"), the internal rhyme ("sand" and three occurrences of "and"). But the most subtle sound effect in this haunting stanza is the tantalizingly approximate rhyme of "anemone" and "enemy".

Through the death of the girl, the fisherman is freed from erotic dreams of "Mast-high moon-white women naked / Walking in wishes and lovely for shame" and from actual sins of the flesh. But, since he has cast his bait, he must wind the reel. He does so "With no more desire than a ghost". The long, melancholy *o's* seem to emphasize his slowness and reluctance. Hauling in the unwelcome catch, the fisherman discovers a child, for "Time [has born] ... another son". He realizes that, ironically enough, he has *not* escaped the monotonous commonplaceness of physical existence, but is inextricably involved in the cycle of birth and death. For the first time, he begins to understand that both the cause and the result of his passion is the inescapable flesh.

From stanza XL on, Thomas universalizes the fisherman's problem of a quest for experience above and beyond the physical. The stanzas skillfully evoke images of disparate civilizations and eras. Worksheets for "The Ballad of the Long-legged Bait" indicate that Thomas consciously merged time and space, ages and places, for the manuscript shows he made specific notations to himself of "times and places" — a phrase he actually uses in stanza XLIV — and of "history dirge".[14] His successful fusion of con-

---

[14] Lita Hornick, "The Intricate Image: A Study of Dylan Thomas". Unpublished Ph. D. dissertation, Columbia University (1958), p. 213.

trasting images is perhaps best illustrated in the resounding line

O Rome and Sodom To-morrow and London.

As the poem itself reveals, Thomas intended this line to suggest
both Sodom and Gomorrah. Since the narrative in Genesis 18
is well known and since Sodom and Gomorrah are usually linked
together, Thomas felt that he could follow "Sodom" by the meaningful rhyme for "Gomorrah", "Tomorrow", and could depend
upon the reader to understand the association. Thus the word
"To-morrow" links the past to the future through verbal association
and denotation. Euphonious and soaring, the line is complex in
its interlocking auditory arrangements. Two vowel sounds are
used two and three times, respectively, within the line: æ in "*a*nd",
"*a*nd"; *o* in "*O*," "R*o*me", "To-morr*o*w". The predominant consonantal patterns are voiced continuants: *r* and *l* for initial sounds
in syllables, *m* and *n* for terminal sounds in syllables:

O *R*o*m*e and Sodo*m* To-*m*orrow and *L*ondon.

Such facets of Thomas's technique in these lines help to make it
reverberate with sound and sense.

In the closing lines, the fisherman returns home, only to find
himself

> ... lost on the land.
> He stands alone at the door of his home,
> With his long-legged heart in his hand.

Through his experience, the fisherman gained a cosmic insight and
a private conscience. Now, though he is "lost on the land", he has
been redeemed through his bride's sacrifice.

XVI

"The Hunchback in the Park", originally written in 1932, was
not published until 1941. Like "The hand that signed the paper",
first composed in 1933, this poem is distinguished by its objectivity
and clarity. But "The Hunchback in the Park" is, for Thomas,
remarkable too in its direct narrative basis.

The structure of the poem is seven stanzas of six lines each with a rather irregular syllabic pattern:

Stanza	Number of Syllables in Each Line
I	6 7 7 10 9 10
II	8 8 8 11 8 7
III	8 7 8 7 9 4
IV	6 8 6 9 6 7
V	6 8 8 9 8 8
VI	7 8 5 8 7 6
VII	7 9 8 11 6 7

Like the syllabic pattern, the speech-stress pattern is irregular; yet the two do not run exactly parallel. Many lines are fairly regular iambic verse; others have truncated or inverted beginnings with, sometimes, anapestic measures within the line. Occasionally — as in stanza II, lines 6 and 7 — the stress pattern is common ballad meter. But such a regular pattern is seldom sustained. The beginnings of certain lines deserve special comment. Stanzas II, III, and IV are linked by several syntactical repetitions in initial positions. That is, present participles open several lines: "Eating", "Drinking", "Running", "Laughing", and "Dodging". The emphasis on these words is increased by their initial position, by their similar meter (usually trochaic), and by their accumulative effect.

The relationships of final words in the lines of the poem vary. Five stanzas have one instance each of full rhyme: in stanza I, "cup", "up"; in stanza III, "down", "town"; in stanza IV, "rockery", "mockery"; in stanzas I and VII — binding the beginning and end of the poem together — "park" and "dark". Other line-end words are approximate rhymes: "lock", "park", "dark"; "early", "clearly"; and the very arresting off-rhyme "shrubberies", "strawberries". Most of the other line-end words are related by final consonance.

Coming early, when the park is opened, and staying late, till it is closed, a solitary hunchback seeks to enjoy the natural beauty of the gardens. The melancholy calmness the hunchback experiences in the park is reflected in the frequency (in stressed positions in the stanza) of the dark, open vowels *a* and *ɔ*: "park", "solitary", "propped", "garden", "lock", "sombre", and "dark". In the park he feels at one with the birds, the trees, and the water, until the taunts and mimicry of the town boys interrupt his musings. The following lines show how the natural, subtle rhythm of the poem corresponds to the meaning. The deformed man is teased and chased by "the truant boys from the town" who begin

> Running when he had heard them clearly
> On out of sound.

The smooth, fast-moving tempo of the first line is created mainly by the quality of the consonants — most of the important consonants are voiced continuants — and by the ratio of unstressed to stressed speech syllables (2:1). The tempo of the first line, like the tempo of the boys' retreat, runs swiftly on. In the second line — the shortest in the poem — the heavily stressed first syllable ("On") is followed by the assonantal echo of "out" and "sound". Here the ratio of unstressed to stressed speech syllables is 1:4, and the rhythm seems to signify the stressed footfalls, which fade away like echoes.

When the boys are gone and the hunchback is alone "between nurses and swans", he creates a fantasy image of a young woman who is tall and straight as the trees and who is free to remain always among the beauties of the park. The hunchback's daydream is first described by the quiet, slow, and lyrical music of the passage

> Made all day until bell time
> A woman figure without fault.

In the first line, the long, lonely day of dreaming is suggested by the slow rhythm of five speech-stressed syllables out of seven syllables, by the long vowels (*e*, *ai*), and by the patterned consonants which emphasize the voiced continuant *l*:

> Made all day until bell time.

And the second line is tightly organized in its cross-alliteration of *w, f, w, f* sounds: "A woman figure without fault". The dominant *l*

sound of the opening line — which is associated with the hunchback's dream — is echoed later in this stanza ("elm", "tall",
"locks") and in the final stanza ("All", "railings", "lake", "wild",
"followed", "kennel"). The perfectly formed woman is, however,
only a vision, an ideal counterpart for the man's crooked shape.
And in the final line of the poem the continuant *l*, like the vision
itself, fades away. Reality closes in, as the park shuts the hunchback
out and the boys chase him to his kennel abode. The harshness
of real life seems enhanced by the frequent use of the explosive *k*
in "hunchback", "kennel", and "dark".

Throughout the poem, the idea of the restless wandering of
the hunchback is supported by the long, meandering poetic statements which continue through several lines and even several
stanzas. Internally, not a single punctuation mark interrupts the
rhythmic flow of the poem. Stanzas I, II, V, and VI have no
punctuated pauses at all; stanzas II, IV, and VII have, respectively,
only a period at the end of the last line of the stanza.

The hunchback's solitary, miserable plight is presented starkly
and quietly, but insistently, and the poem is devoid of sentimentality
and flamboyant tone. Moreover, the contrasting sound patterns
seem to highlight the fundamental difference between the hunchback's ideal and real existence.

XVII

"Ceremony After a Fire Raid" is a melodic dirge (for a newborn
infant who was "burned to tireless death" in a fire raid) and a
ritualistic celebration of renewal of life. The form of the poem,
although loose, has, within each of the first two parts — the third
part has only one section —, a relatively regular syllabic count:

	Stanza	Number of Syllables in Each Line
Part I	I	2 3 1 9 6 5 8 10
	II	2 3 1 10 7 5 9 12
	III	2 3 – 10 7 5 8 11
	IV	2 8 1 9 7 6 8 11

Part II   I   5 11 5 6 4 7 5 9 5 8 5 9 6 7

                II   5 12 6 6 4 7 5 8 5 8 6 9 6 7

The expanding form of the entire poem compares roughly to musical crescendos. A glance at the printed text of the poem makes that statement obvious. For in the first part each stanza begins with lines of a few syllables and builds up to a line of ten to twelve syllables; in the second part the lines of each stanza are longer than most of those in the first part; in the third part the lines are longer than most of those in the second part.

As an opening phrase, "Myselves / The grievers / Grieve" is singularly arresting. The coinage "Myselves" immediately binds the reader, Thomas, and other grievers together in a communal yet deeply personal lament for an innocent child's death. Part of the musical effectiveness of the phrase can be explained by the fact that the graphs of the striking power, vowel tone, and pitch are relatively parallel:

Striking Power

Vowel Tone

Pitch

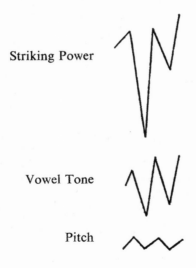

Each stanza in part I opens with two or three short lines that include a repetition of a key word in the thematic development of that stanza: "grieve" (stanza I), "sing" (stanza II), "forgive" (stanza III), "cry" (stanza IV). It is interesting to note that, when the word is repeated, it is varied by a slight alteration in its form or by a change in its metrical position in the line. For example, in stanza III the first line is the single word "Forgive", and the speech stress is iambic; the same word is repeated in the second line, "Us forgive", but the speech stress now is the converse of an amphibrach. This stress pattern is the more meaningful since the first two lines of stanzas I, II, and IV are an iamb followed by an amphibrach. Because the word "Us" is stressed and is in an initial position in both lines 2 and 3, the reader's involvement in the "ceremony" is secured. The conclusion of line 3 of this stanza forms an ingenious link with the poem's opening lines, in that "myselves the believers" echoes the earlier "Myselves / The grievers". Such echoes unify and intensify the strong musical qualities of the poem.

Neither grieving nor singing, the poem asserts, can bring life out of death. And even if a miracle could do so, the "Darkness kindled back into beginning" would not atone for the child's death. All that can now be done is to beg the child's forgiveness of the sin committed against it and to believe that "Love is the last light spoken". Part II deepens the sacrificial aspect of the child's death, which was suggested early in the poem with the symbolism of the child's "arms full of fires". The child's burning is, in the second part, associated with all deaths and sacrificial ceremonies since Adam and Eve. And the idyllic, ancient garden of Eden is contrasted with the sinful, modern "garden of wilderness", in which "Beginning crumbled back to darkness". Not only is this line forceful in its repetition of the explosive *b* sound and its approximate rhyme of "back" and "dark-", but it is also meaningful in its inversion of the prayerful chant of the mourners in stanza II: "Darkness kindled back into beginning." Moreover, the verb in each line, though different in meaning, is similar in sound ("kindled" and "crumbled"). The subtle relationship of these lines and their overtones of Genesis I:1-5 make it clear that Thomas probably intended a double and implied antithesis of light and darkness, of beginning and end, in each line. Thus the symbolism of life and death is underscored.

In commenting on the poem to Vernon Watkins, Thomas said, "It really is a Ceremony, and the third part of the poem is the music

at the end. Would it be called a voluntary, or is that only music at
the beginning?" His query about a voluntary — which is especially
associated with an *organ* solo in a church service — and the reference
in the first line of part III to "organpipes" lead one to suspect that
Thomas consciously wrote this stanza as a poetry of full organ
tones. The sheer evocativeness of this passage, particularly when
spoken aloud, is hardly matched in contemporary literature. The
alliterative phrases at the ends of the lines are very impressive:
"*m*olten *m*ouths", "*d*itch of *d*aybreak", "*b*urning like *b*randy".
The entire stanza *does* seem to be one uninterrupted organ postlude,
hinting — through the allusions to the bread and wine of Holy
Communion — at purification and redemption for all, through the
child's sacrifice. The finale is climaxed by the hope that man can

> Erupt, fountain, and enter to utter for ever
> Glory glory glory
> The sundering ultimate kingdom of genesis' thunder.

With its five occurrences of the explosive *t* sound, the first line is
extremely expressive and forceful. The concluding phrase, "enter
to utter for ever", sets in relief the five explosives, because all the
stressed words begin with a vowel. Further, the three instances of
words ending in the final -*er* sound ("enter", "utter", "for ever")
evoke the idea of repetition.[15] In the second line the resounding
"Glory glory glory" corresponds to the "Holy holy holy" of the
Christian church service. Like the speech stresses of the phrase
"and enter to utter for ever", those of the final line are in perfectly
regular amphibrachs. The suggestions of infinite repetitions (in
the -*er* sound of "sunder-" and "thunder") and the assonance of
the solid ʌ sound (in "s*u*ndering *u*ltimate" and "th*u*nder") contribute to the powerful, majestic organ chords of the line. The
rhyme, which is both internal and line-end — "The masses of the
sea *under*" and "The *sunder*ing ... *thunder*" — help make the concluding passage one long, glorious reverberation. Thus a dirge for

---

[15]   Consider, for example, other words with final -*er* sounds which indicate
repetition: "jabber", "chatter", "whisper", "clatter", "mutter", "sputter",
"flicker", "shimmer", etc.

a newborn infant has resolved magnificently into a paean of hope for

>The sundering ultimate kingdom of genesis' thunder.

XVIII

Over a span of twelve years, Thomas wrote three poems celebrating, respectively, his twenty-fourth, thirtieth, and thirty-fifth birthdays: "Twenty-four years remind the tears of my eyes", "Poem in October", and "Poem on his Birthday". The first poem is representative of Thomas's best poetry in his first poetic period, the second in his second poetic period, and the third in his third poetic period.[16]

"Poem in October" is an elegiac reminiscence of the lost innocence and joy of childhood. Appropriately enough, the stanzas are long and complex, usually consisting of a single sentence; this form corresponds to the leisurely drift of a reverie of the past. There are seven stanzas of ten lines each. The poem is, moreover, beautifully patterned in its syllabic line:

Stanza	Number of Syllables in Each Line[17]									
I	*10*	12	9	3	5	12	12	5	3	9
II	9	12	9	3	5	12	12	5	3	9
III	9	12	9	3	5	12	12	5	3	9
IV	9	12	9	3	5	12	12	5	3	9
V	9	12	9	3	5	12	12	5	3	9
VI	9	12	9	3	5	*13*	12	5	3	9
VII	9	12	9	3	*6*	12	12	5	3	9

The pattern of speech stresses is varied. One aspect of the pattern should, however, be discussed. The line-end words form a special

[16] If a recording of Thomas reading "Twenty-four years" had been available, a comparative study would have been made of the three birthday poems as representatives of their respective poetic periods.

[17] Ralph N. Maud shows — in "Language and Meaning in the Poetry of Dylan Thomas". Unpublished Ph. D. dissertation, Harvard University (1958), p. 151 — the syllabic count to reveal only one irregularity (the one in stanza VI). But since Thomas pronounces the word "thirtieth" on the recording as three rather than two syllables, there is also an irregularity in stanzas I and VII, where that word occurs.

rhythmic pattern. In the following table, *m* represents the masculine line-end words, *f* represents the feminine line-end words, and *d* represents the dactylic line-end words.

Stanza   Rhythm of the Line-end Words[18]

Stanza										
I	f	m	f	m	f	m	m	m	f	m
II	f	m	f	m	f	m	m	f	m	m
III	f	f	f	d	f	d	f	f	m	d
IV	f	m	f	m	f	m	m	f	f	m
V	f	m	f	f	f	m	f	d	f	f
VI	d	m	m	m	d	m	m	d	m	m
VII	f	m	f	m	d	m	m	m	m	f

The initial and final assonance and the similar rhythm of the three dactylic line-end words in stanza III closely bind them together: "Summery", "suddenly", and "under me". The entire stanza seems especially light and airy, because — in contrast to the comparatively heavy masculine line-end words which dominate the first two stanzas — the line-end words, with one exception, are all fluid feminine or dactylic words.

For three years before he finished it, Thomas contemplated "Poem in October". When he mailed a copy to Vernon Watkins he said, "I do hope you like it, & wd like very much to read it aloud to you. Will you read it aloud too? It's got, I think, a lovely slow lyrical movement."[19] Thomas was right. The poem demands oral reading. And, fortunately, a superb reading by Thomas is preserved on a commercial recording. Listening to it, one can best realize the slow, lyrical rhythm which Thomas achieved in the poem.

In the airy opening stanza to "Poem in October" —

It was my thirtieth year to heaven
Woke to my hearing from harbour and neighbor wood

[18] Note that when the line-end word is not heavily stressed — as in line 10, stanza III and in line 9, stanza V — the final phrase is taken into consideration in order to determine the rhythm. (In line 10, stanza VI, the line-end word, "singingbirds", hovers between masculine and dactylic rhythm, but Thomas's reading does slightly accent the final syllable and thus makes the word masculine.)
[19] *LVW*, pp. 115-116.

> And the mussel pooled and the heron
> Priested shore
> The morning beckon
> With water praying and call of seagull and rook
> And the knock of sailing boats on the net webbed wall
> Myself to set foot
> That second
> In the still sleeping town and set forth.

— the poet is enveloped in the sights and sounds of the October day, which are described in an inimitable word magic. Witness the subtle, interlocking repetitions in the line

Woke to my hearing from harbour and neighbor wood

or the net of auditory arrangements in "net webbed wall". In the line-end words of four of the ten lines, the intricate sound relation-ships reflect more than simple assonance: "heaven" and "heron" are identical in all except the initial and medial consonants; "beckon" and "second" are identical except for the initial and final cosnonants. Notice also the internal full rhymes ("year", "hear-" and "net", "set") and approximate rhymes ("call", "-gull" and "rook", "knock") and assonance ("wood", "rook", "foot").

Rising early on the rainy autumn morning of his thirtieth birth-day, the poet sets out on a walk "in a shower of all my days," in a reverie of his past. The gates of the present close behind him as he crosses the border into the past:

> High tide and the heron dived when I took the road
> Over the border
> And the gates
> Of the town closed as the town awoke.

The musical effect of the opening phrase in ingenious. In addition to the assonance of the *ai* sound in "High", "tide", and "dived", there is consonance in "High" "heron", and "tide" "dived". And the last three lines — echoing the earlier assonance of "water", "horses", "rose", and "road" — close the passage slowly, because of the concentrated accumulations of the long vowel *o* in "Over", "border", "closed", and "awoke".

In stanzas III and IV the poet ascends the summit of happy
childhood memories, where the October weather has, in his
imagination, turned to the summer of sun and rolling clouds, of
birds and blooming gardens. Yet below him remains the brown
and autumnal present, with

>   ... the rain wringing
>   Wind blow[ing] cold
>   In the wood faraway under me.

The phrase "rain wringing / Wind" is saturated with phonetic
echoes: the alliteration of the continuant *r* ("*r*ain w*r*inging"); the
frequency of the nasals *n* and *ŋ* ("rai*n* wri*ng*ing / Wi*nd*"); the
internal rhyme ("-inging"); the assonance of the clear vowel *ɪ*
("wr*i*nging / W*i*nd"). The impression here of a gentle, even patter
of an autumnal shower is created by the repeated use of the short,
clear vowel *ɪ*. In striking contrast is the phrase which follows it,
"blow cold", with its repetition of the prolongable, dark vowel *o*
Combined with the use of the explosive *b* and *k* sounds, this phrase
correlates with the idea of cold gusts of wind.

As the poet muses, his reverie seems for the moment to become
reality. For the "weather turned around", and he is able once
again to feel "the other air" and to see "the blue altered sky" of
the golden days of his youth. In this "wonder of summer" he
relives the

>   Forgotten mornings when he walked with his mother
>   Through the parables
>   Of sun light
>   And the legends of the green chapels.

The prodigiously involved vowel and consonantal arrangements
of this stanza — and, indeed, of the entire poem — complement
its deepest emotional meaning, *harmony*. Exceedingly delicate
relationships between words permeate the poem. For example,
the closely juxtaposed words "wonder" and "summer" are related
through assonance and through rhymed unstressed final syllables.
Further, the widely separated line-end words "apples" and "chapels"
are related by full rhyme, and both words, by approximate rhyme,
are linked to another line-end word, "parables". (In turn, "parables"

is associated by assonance and initial consonance to "pears".)
The sounds, then, are harmoniously interrelated. Similarly, the
poet and the spirit of the child become as one: "his tears burned
my cheeks and his heart moved in mine". The poet realizes that
"the long dead child" is a part of the wonder of nature and that his
spirit communicates "the truth of his joy" to trees, stones, and fish.
The effect of unity is heightened by such auditory echoes as the
rhyming of the initial syllables in "*lis*tening", "*whis*pered", and
"*mys*tery". Everywhere the wonder of nature is evident, for

> ... the mystery
> Sang alive
> Still in the water and singingbirds.

In the final stanza the poet, still feeling the child's joy "burning
in the sun", prays for his future ability to recapture and respond to
the lost innocence and joy of childhood, to experience again
unparalleled unity and harmony:

> O may my heart's truth
> Still be sung
> On this high hill in a year's turning.

XIX

"A Refusal to Mourn the Death, by Fire, of a Child in London"
is a short, twenty-four-line poem of four stanzas of six lines each.
The syllabic count reveals an irregular pattern:

Stanza	Number of Syllables in Each Line					
I	9	5	9	9	5	10
II	9	7	10	10	5	10
III	11	5	11	10	5	9
IV	10	5	10	9	5	10

The rhyme scheme, however, is one of Thomas's most regular, for
it follows the pattern *abcabc*, with the short lines in the stanza
rhyming *bb*. In the first stanza all the rhyme words are feminine,
since Thomas pronounces "flower" and "hour" each as two
syllables. In the second stanza all the rhyme words are masculine.

In stanzas III and IV all the feminine rhymes are words ending in
-*er*. Only three pairs of rhymes are approximate: "darkness",
"harness"; "murder", "further"; "friends", "Thames". All the rest
are full rhymes. Notwithstanding such regularity and repetition,
the rhymes are not immediately apparent upon a first reading or
first listening. In contrast to most of the poems in Thomas's early
poetic period (in which the lines are mainly end-stopped and sense-
determined), this poem is characterized by enjambment, which
naturally de-emphasizes the rhyme words. As to internal rhyme,
two instances occur: "*humbling* darkness" and "*tumbling* in harness",
a situation which makes up for the only approximate quality of the
end-rhyme in these lines; and "grains" and "veins", whose long
vowels contribute to the slow, melancholy effect of "The grains
beyond age, the dark veins of her mother."

The pattern of speech-stressed syllables in "A Refusal to Mourn"
is varied. Yet in each stanza a complex pattern is repeated in
similar portions of different lines. In stanza I the phrases "mankind
making" and "last light breaking" form a spondee followed by a
trochee; the identical rhythm, in addition to the assonance in
"kind" and "light", reinforces the full rhyme. In stanza II, lines
1 and 4 are rhythmically identical — except for an initial (and
extra) unstressed syllable in line 4 — in forming an iamb followed
by an amphibrach followed by two iambs:

> And I must enter again the round
> . . . .
> And the synagogue of the ear of corn.

In stanza III, lines 1 and 3, the concluding phrases are identical in
rhythm: "burning of the child's death" and "going with a grave
truth". Line 4 lacks the extra stressed syllable with which lines 1
and 3 conclude, but otherwise it, too, has the same rhythm:
"stations of the breath". In stanza IV the first and last lines are
metrically identical, with a dactyl followed by a spondee followed
by two iambs plus an unstressed final syllable:

> Deep with the first dead lies London's daughter
> . . . .
> After the first death, there is no other.

In regard to the speech stresses, however, only the first seven syllables are rhythmically the same, since on the recording Thomas accents the word "no". In several cases in which the rhythmic pattern is similar, the phrases also bear similar syntactical constructions (e.g., "burning of the child's death" and "going with a grave truth") or auditory repetitions (e.g., "first dead" and "first death"). Such parallelisms further help to bind parts of the poem intricately together.

Especially the first three stanzas of "A Refusal to Mourn" contain few punctuated pauses. Instead, these stanzas form a series of long rhetorical units, as in the opening lines:

> Never until the mankind making
> Bird beast and flower
> Fathering and all humbling darkness
> . . . .

Although this swiftly-flowing introduction is interesting in the cross-alliteration of *m* and *k* sounds and in the scattered assonance, it is in the lines following that some of the most intriguing and complex consonantal arrangements in the poem appear:

> *Tells* with *silence* the *last light* breaking
> And the *still* hour.

Aside from the assonance in "silence" and "light", the variations upon the sounds *s*, *t*, and *l* singly or in combination are remarkable. The concentration of these sounds culminates in the adjective "still", which (because of the frequency, in the preceding line, of its three consonantal sounds) is heavily emphasized. Since by uttering the word "silence", silence is broken and by uttering the word "still", stillness is broken, auditory effects cannot really correlate with these concepts, but can only indicate related concepts. Usually silence and stillness are related to softness and slowness. And here the suggestion of silence and stillness is conveyed by the softness and slowness created by the combinations of sounds used in these lines.

Throughout the lyric, the poet elaborates upon a general theme: that he will not mourn needlessly the death of those who are

absorbed into the mystery of Nature. In particular, he will not
make an elegy for the innocent youth who died in a London fire,
for she has escaped the deaths-in-life which the long-lived experience; she will die only the one time. The poet expresses this
conclusion in the closing line, "After the first death, there is no
other", which is memorable for at least two reasons. First, it is
a succinct statement complete within one line. Since the poem is,
for the most part, composed of long, rhetorical units spanning
as much as thirteen lines, the clarity and compression of this
final line is, by contrast, enhanced. Secondly, the literal clarity of the
line veils an ambiguous implication. Specifically, does "After the
first death, there is no other" imply a pessimistic philosophy of
mortality, or a Christian philosophy of immortality?

XX

"A Winter's Tale" is considered by several critics, including
David Daiches and W. S. Merwin, to be one of Thomas's most
magnificent poems. Probably greater restraint would make for
more enduring criticism. For, in all likelihood, "A Winter's Tale"
is simply Thomas's most beautifully sustained and unified long
narrative poem. A comparison between "A Winter's Tale" and
"The Ballad of the Long-legged Bait" illuminates this qualified
praise of the poem. On the one hand, the narrative of "A Winter's
Tale" — which may well be based upon myth — lends itself to a
single symbolic interpretation (i.e., a winter ceremony of the rebirth
of man and nature) better than does the narrative of the mysterious
voyage of a fisherman whose bride is his bait. The imagery of
"A Winter's Tale" is more precisely handled and its rich and sustained musical texture more pervasive than in "The Ballad". On
the other hand, "The Ballad" seems superior in the interesting
variety of its rhymes (e.g., "anemone" and "enemy") and in the
exquisite lyricism of individual passages (e.g., "O Rome and Sodom
To-morrow and London"). At its best, portions of "The Ballad"
surpass the beauty of "A Winter's Tale", but in its total unity and
sustained lyricism, "A Winter's Tale" is the more nearly perfect

poem. Thomas struggled long to achieve unity in "A Winter's Tale" and, in writing to Vernon Watkins, expressed his feeling that, after all, he had fallen short of his aim: "I'm sending you some new poems. The long one ["A Winter's Tale"] doesn't, I think, come off, but I like it all in spite of that. It isn't really one piece, though, God, I tried to make it one and have been working on it for months."[20]

As to structure, "A Winter's Tale" has twenty-six stanzas of five lines each. Only the first lines of each stanza have the same syllabic count; that is, each of them except the one in the twenty-sixth stanza has six syllables. But throughout the poem, even in the six-syllable first lines of the stanzas, the speech stresses vary considerably. The line-end word scheme, however, is in a strict pattern of *ababa*. Over half the rhymes are full rhymes and, up to the thirteenth stanza, the approximate rhymes all involve the addition or omission of a *z* sound:

Stanza		Stanza	
I	tale, sail, vales lakes, flakes	VII	stones, bones, alone_ sky, sties
II	cold, hold, told owl, cowl	VIII	prayers, lairs, air_ cloud, bowed
III	old, unrolled, fold bread, head	IX	strung, tongues, among tossed, lost
IV	then, hen, men snow, crow	X	night, white, light caught, sought
V	spades, milkmaids, trades shy, sky	XI	cried, bride, astride need, seed
VI	prayed, shade, afraid light, night	XII	sing, wings, spring nightingale, tale

In the remainder of the poem, the addition or omission of a *z* sound is never responsible for the approximate rhymes. It is as if the poem more or less progressed from regularity in rhyme to greater and more frequent irregularities, such as the approximate rhymes like "look" linked with "rock" and "flock". Repetition of the same rhyme-base occurs throughout the poem. For example,

[20] *LVW*, p. 126.

two rhyme-bases are each used four times: the rhyme-base
"light", in stanzas VI, X, XV, XVIII and the rhyme base "bride",
in stanzas XI, XIV, XXI, XXV. Other rhyme-bases are also
repeated: "old" in stanzas II, III, and XVI; "snow" in stanzas
IV, XIX, and XXVI; "bread" in stanzas III and XXIII; "lakes"
in stanzas I and XX; "tale" in stanzas I and XII; "sky" in stanzas V
and VII. The recurrence of these particular rhymes — many of
which are words concerned with nature — contributes to the
pastoral qualities of the poem.

The narrative of "A Winter's Tale" opens with a quiet but vivid
description of snow falling over the countryside and of a man at his
farmhouse fireside watching the outdoor wintry scene. In his
recording, Thomas reads the first three stanzas softly; but even
without the benefit of his reading, a sensitive reader of the printed
passage knows that its music somehow falls almost as softly as the
snow itself. The few consonantal clusters in the first three stanzas
involve primarily continuants. The occurrences in the passage of
the rather intense *f* sound are softened by the many *l* sounds:
"ta*l*e", "b*l*ind", "twi*l*ight", "*l*akes", "*fl*oating fie*l*ds", "va*l*es",
"G*l*iding wind*l*ess", "fo*l*ded *fl*akes", "pa*l*e", "catt*l*e", "stea*l*thy
sai*l*", to list only those in the first stanza. The quiet effect of the
passage is enhanced, too, by the almost effortless initial semi-
vowels in some words (for instance, "*v*ales", "*w*indless", "*W*arning",
"*w*ended *v*ales", and "*w*orld") and the almost effortless final vowel
sounds in other words (for instance, "sn*ow*", "thr*ough*", "h*ay*",
and "sn*ow*"). These varied facets of Thomas's auditory technique
account largely for the sound echoing the sense in the opening three
stanzas.

In marked contrast is the passage in stanza VI:

> He knelt, he wept, he prayed,
> By the spit and the black pot in the log bright light
> And the cup and the cut bread....

Here the final consonants in all the important words are explosives
("knel*t*", "we*pt*", "praye*d*", "spi*t*", "blac*k* po*t*", "lo*g* brigh*t* lig*ht*",
"cu*p*", and "cu*t* brea*d*"). The fact that the twenty-five words of
the passage are all monosyllables further contributes to the staccato
effect. By the clipped sounds in the line "By the spit and the black

pot in the log bright light", Thomas must have intended to evoke
the idea of a crackling, cozy fireside, for in stanza XVIII he repeats
the phrase, again against a background of more legato sounds
describing the serene wintry scene.

The following stanza (XIV) is selected to illustrate the typical
complexity of vowel and consonantal arrangements in "A Winter's
Tale".

It was a hand or sound
In the long ago land that glided the dark door wide
And there outside on the bread of the ground
A she bird rose and rayed like a burning bride.
A she bird dawned, and her breast with snow and scarlet downed.

In addition to the full end rhyme ("sound", "ground", "downed"
and "wide", "bride"), there is internal rhyme ("hand", "land" and
"glided", "wide", "outside", "bride"). Further, final consonance
of the *d* sound permeates the stanza: "han*d*", "soun*d*", "lan*d*",
"glide*d*", "wi*d*e", "outsi*d*e", "brea*d*", "groun*d*", "bir*d*", "raye*d*",
"bri*d*e", "bir*d*", "dawne*d*", and "downe*d*". All these words, except
"glided" and "outside," are monosyllables. Many of them are
linked by other means than simply final consonance — for example,
"rayed" and "bride" as well as "dawned" and "downed". A concentration of the consonants *b* and *r* near the end-rhyme "*br*ide"
heightens its semantic importance: "*br*ead", "*b*i*r*d", "*b*u*r*ning",
"*b*i*r*d", and "*br*east". Internal elements and line-end words weave
a web of assonance and alliteration. Moreover, stanza XIV is
representative of the poem as a whole in its harmony of sound and
sense.

Thus "A Winter's Tale" is to a great degree a unified and sustained poem because of its rich musical texture, achieved through
ingenious repetitions of consonants, vowels, and even entire rhyme-
bases. In this poem phonetic devices seem employed more extensively, if less memorably, than in most of Thomas's poetry.

XXI

Like "Poem in October", the lyric "Fern Hill" laments the loss of childhood joy and innocence by recreating childhood spontaneity and implying both its transience and its contrast with the poet's adult existence.

Thomas's craft in "Fern Hill" is intricate. Not only is the poem well-patterned in its structure, six stanzas of nine lines each, but it is also well-patterned in its syllabic count. The first, second, third, and fifth stanzas are perfectly regular; the fourth, sixth, and seventh have one irregularity each; and the eighth and ninth contain, in identical positions, two different syllabic counts:[21]

Stanza	Number of Syllables in Each Line								
I	14	14	9	6	9	*15*	14	7	9
II	14	14	9	6	9	14	14	7	9
III	14	14	9	*5*	9	14	14	*9*	*6*
IV	14	14	9	6	9	14	14	*9*	*6*
V	14	14	9	6	9	14	14	*9*	*6*
VI	14	14	9	6	9	14	*15*	7	9

The rhythm of the poem flows with the long, lilting lines, which are associated primarily with lightheartedness of youth, and ebbs with the short, slower lines, which are associated primarily with the sinister presence of time. More specifically, although the patterns of the speech stresses vary widely throughout the poem, certain tendencies in the speech stresses distinguish the long lines from the short lines. For the most part, the long lines have less than a 1:2 ratio of stressed to unstressed syllables, whereas the short lines — line 4 of each stanza and line 8 of stanzas I, II, and VI and line 9 of stanzas III, IV, and V — usually have a 1:2 ratio. The lilting quality of the long lines is further heightened by the frequent anapestic beginnings; the more somber quality of the short lines, by the frequent heavily stressed beginnings.

The assonance of the stressed syllables of the line-end words in the poem helps to produce a singing, chanting effect. The assonantal arrangements are in the pattern *abcddabcd*:

---

[21] In effect, then, the second very short line in each stanza is simply placed as line 9, rather than line 8, in stanzas III, IV, and V.

Stanza   Stanza

   I boughs, town   IV white, light
      green, leaves   all, warm
      starry, barley   maiden, stable
      climb, eyes, light   again, day, praise
  II barns, calves   V house, allows
      home, cold   long, songs
      only, slowly   over, golden
      be, means, streams   ways, hay, grace
 III hay, away   VI me, means
      air, night-jars   hand, land
      watery, horses   rising, dying
      grass, stars, dark   sleep, fields, sea

There are only three types of departures from the *abcddabcd* pattern of assonance: (1) one instance of only approximate assonance, in "air" and "night-jars"; (2) one instance of Thomas's pronunciation (on the recording) making approximate assonance of what can be pronounced as full assonance, in "again" — which Thomas reads with a stressed ε vowel — with "day" and "praise"; (3) one instance of a change in the assonantal pattern, in stanza VI, where it becomes *abcddbacd*. The rhythm of the line-end words forms a very distinctive scheme. With the exception of the final phrase, "take me," in stanza VI, line 1, all line-end words are feminine in lines 3 and 8 and masculine in the other lines.

A very important but seldom mentioned factor in the lilt of the lines in "Fern Hill" is the high frequency of vowels. An examination reveals that there is often a fairly continuous alternation of vowel and consonantal sounds and that, when consonants *are* juxtaposed, they are in several instances lightly breathed *h's*, as in "*h*ay / Fields *h*igh as the *h*ouse" or "*h*appy as the *h*eart was long", or semi-vowels, as in "the sun that is *y*oung once only" or "the spellbound horses *w*alking *w*arm." In the opening lines of stanza II, many of the words begin or end in a vowel sound:

   *A*nd *a*s *I* was green *a*nd carefr*ee*, famous *a*mong th*e* barns
   *A*bout th*e* happ*y* yard *a*nd singing *a*s th*e* farm was home,
     *I*n th*e* sun that *i*s young once onl*y*,

> Time let me play and be
> Golden in the mercy of his means.

Note that a nasal — mostly preceded by the ʌ vowel — links the semantically important words in the line "In the sun that is young once only."

So superbly constructed is "Fern Hill" that the symbolic imagery and the sound patterns in every line contribute to the balanced and unified whole. Consider, for example, the first stanza.

> Now as I was young and easy under the apple boughs
> About the lilting house and happy as the grass was green,
>> The night above the dingle starry,
>> Time let me hail and climb
>> Golden in the heydays of his eyes,
> And honoured among wagons I was prince of the apple towns
> And once below a time I lordly had the trees and leaves
>> Trail with daisies and barley
> Down the rivers of the windfall light.

The opening words, "Now as I was young and easy", hint, through the use of the past tense, of the loss of youthful bliss, and the phrase "Time let me hail and climb" suggests that time rules even the child's life. Moreover, the phrase "once below a time" (used to less advantage in a poem by that title) not only evokes the familiar fairy-tale introduction, but also poignantly underscores the fact that the child is subject to the laws of time. In the light of these ominous suggestions, which are made more explicit in the later stanzas, the child's sovereignty, as the "prince of the apple towns" who "lordly had the trees", is charged with irony. Yet for the moment, all seems green and golden, and the child is an integral part of his environment. Throughout the stanza, alliteration (such as "grass was green"), assonance (such as "trees and leaves"), and internal rhyme or near-rhyme (such as "apple", "happy" and "Time", "climb") create a euphony which aptly reinforces the emotional meaning of the harmony between the child and nature.

In the second stanza the rhythmical swing of the long lines describes further the happy, carefree childhood on the farm; the slower pace of the short lines again emphasizes the somber, inevitable changes. Especially effective is the syntactical repetition beginning in the fourth line ("Time let me be / Golden...") which balances the phrase beginning in the fourth line of the first stanza ("Time let me hail and climb / Golden..."). In stanza III the opening tempo runs fast with lightly stressed rhythms, syntactical repetitions, and consonance of the smooth continuant *l* ("it was *lovely* ... it was air / And p*l*aying, *lovely* and watery"). But the succeeding lines foreshadow the conclusion of the poem, when the delights of childhood are lost forever; for here the delights of childhood are temporarily borne away during the night. This portentous event is, fittingly enough, described with dark vowels (in "r*o*de", "*ow*ls", "m*oo*n l*o*ng", and "h*o*rses"). In stanza IV the farm has returned with the dew, and the flowing phrase of stanza III is echoed in "it was all / Shining, it was Adam and maiden". So joyous and so innocent were those youthful days that the poet compares them to the first days of Creation:

> So it must have been after the birth of the simple light
> In the first, spinning place, the spellbound horses walking warm,
>> Out of the whinnying green stable
>> On to the fields of praise.

Among the many phonetic echoes in these lyrical lines, two are particularly interesting: the excitingly approximate internal rhyme in "spinning" and "whinnying"; the consecutive and vertical assonance of stressed syllables in "gr*ee*n st*a*ble" and "f*ie*lds of pr*ai*se". Similarly interesting echoes permeate the final stanzas (witness the internal rhyme in stanza VI, line 5, of "I", "fly", "high"). The facts of time become more insistent in the conclusion, but the child is still heedless. The poet makes no moral judgment on the child's attitude; instead, he implies his sorrow that such joy and innocence are transient and his wonder that such beauty and spontaneity ever existed at all:

> Time held me green and dying
> Though I sang in my chains like the sea.

The undeniable magic in "Fern Hill" can never be even partially analyzed. Only Thomas's intricate craft can be. For poetic magic is elusive and, as Thomas himself commented, it is

always accidental. No poet would labour intensively upon the intricate craft of poetry unless he hoped that, suddenly, the accident of magic would occur. He *has* to agree with Chesterton that the miraculous thing about miracles is that they *do* sometimes happen. And the best poem is that whose worked-upon unmagical passages come closest, in texture and intensity, to those moments of magical accident.[22]

Since Thomas spoke these words in a B.B.C. broadcast in June of 1946 and since "Fern Hill" was probably composed sometime the year before, Thomas may have had this poem in mind. That he worked extensively on the poem is attested by the fact that he wrote over two hundred "separate and distinct versions" of it.[23] By his own standard, then, "Fern Hill" is a "best poem". For its "worked-upon unmagical passages" have been transformed mysteriously into a unified poem which is one of the few "moments of magical accident" in contemporary poetry.

XXII

"In my Craft or Sullen Art" is a twenty-line lyric with eleven lines in the first stanza and nine lines in the second stanza. That the second stanza is shorter by two lines has interesting ramifications in respect to the balanced structural patterns of the two stanzas. If the patterns of syllables, of speech stresses, of line-end rhymes, and of line-end rhythms are studied, it becomes obvious that only two lines upset the parallelism between the stanzas. Close observation of the rhyme scheme does, however, make a solution obvious: if, instead of assuming that the two extra lines in stanza I correspond to the last two lines of stanza II, one considers them as the sixth and seventh lines of stanza II, then the pattern appears quite uniform. In the light of this adjustment, the balanced structure of the syllabic pattern, as well as of the speech stresses, becomes evident:

	Number of Syllables in Each Line		Number of Speech-Stresses in Each Line
Stanza		Stanza	
I	7 7 7 7 7 7 7 7 7 7 6	I	4 3 3 3 3 3 3 3 2 3 3
II	7 7 6 7 7 - - 7 7 7 6	II	3 3 4 3 3 - - 3 2 3 3

[22] "On Poetry: A Discussion", *Encounter*, III (November, 1954), p. 25.
[23] John Malcolm Brinnin, *Dylan Thomas in America* (New York, 1958), p. 125.

But an even greater uniformity exists in the rhyme scheme. In all, there are only five rhyme-bases in the poem, since the second stanza uses the same rhyme-bases (and in parallel positions) as the first stanza. And the rhyme schemes of the two stanzas are — with the exception of the omitted lines — identical:

> Stanza I *abcdebdecca*
> II *abcde—ecca*

Even though the lines are very short, the rhymes do not create a "singsong" effect, because most lines are run-on and because each stanza is one long sentence. Since the same rhyme-bases are used in parallel positions in both stanzas, it follows that the pattern of masculine and feminine rhymes is necessarily identical in both stanzas:

> Stanza I m m f m m m m m f f m
> II m m f m m – – m f f m

Syntactical and phrasal repetitions contribute to the structural unity of "In my Craft or Sullen Art". In stanza I occur the introductory words "Not for" (line 7) and "But for" (line 10); in stanza II occur the introductory words "Not for" (line 1), "Nor for" (line 4), "But for" (line 6), and "Nor" (line 9). It is noteworthy that four of these six lines have identical metrical patterns: a trochee followed by an amphibrach followed by an iamb. The line "But for the common wages" differs only in that the rhyme word is a trochee instead of an iamb. The final line of the poem ("Nor heed my craft or art") differs markedly from the other five related lines in its continuous iambic pattern.

Assonance and consonance form an important part of the lyricism of "In my Craft or Sullen Art". In the opening line, for example, the assonance — in Thomas's pronunciation — and the final consonance of the words "craft" and "art" link them in sound and sense. Other effective sound patterns might be pointed out: the consonance of the *s* sound in "sullen", "Exercised", and "still" and of the *n* sound in "sullen", "in", "night", "When only", and "moon"; the assonance in "exercised" and "night"; the alliteration of "lovers lie", which is echoed in "all" in the succeeding line; the use of *s*, *t*, and *r* sounds in "the strut and trade of charms / On the ivory stages", which (by binding together "strut", "trade", and "stages") stresses the suggestion of Shakespeare's "poor player", who "struts and frets his hour upon the stage / And then is heard no more".

But the most euphonious and lyrical line in the first stanza is: "I labour by singing light". Here the first, middle, and last syllables of the line (i.e., "I", "by", and "light") are related by assonance of the long diphthong *ai*. Consonance of *l* and *b* sounds is prominent in "labour by ... light". The word "singing", with its repetition of "-ing", reinforces the effect of the meaning suggested by the first syllable of the word. Moreover, *iŋiŋ* is very light, voiced throughout, and composed entirely of continuants. In the second stanza fewer sound patterns are obvious, so that the three occurrences of the long vowel *e* in "Who pay no praise nor wages" are the more emphatic. Part of the musical effectiveness of the phrase can be explained by the fact that the graphs of the vowel tone and pitch are parallel. Indeed the parallelism continues into the final line and thus connects the closing thoughts of the poem.

Vowel Tone

Pitch

A lyrical *ars poetica*, "In my Craft or Sullen Art" agrees with Thomas's prose statements on his method of composition and his purpose in writing poetry. His poetic craft is a "sullen art" which results not so much from divine inspiration as from constant practice and labor. Yet he feels his craft must be closely related to the inmost heart of real life, i.e., the intense joys and sorrows of

> ... the lovers [who] lie abed
> With all their griefs in their arms.

His art, the poem says, is for the lovers, even though they ignore it. In a prose statement defending the usefulness of his poetry, Thomas had earlier said:

My poetry is ... the record of my individual struggle from darkness towards some measure of light. ... My poetry is, or should be, useful to others for its individual recording of that same struggle with which they are necessarily acquainted.[24]

The lovers, however, "pay no praise or wages / Nor heed my craft or art". Even so, Thomas's poetry is written for them; both his art and the lovers' actions reflect the essential experiences of life.

[24]   *Quite Early One Morning*, p. 188.

CHAPTER III

In Thomas's third and final period, 1946 till his death in 1953, he wrote only eight poems, six of which are analyzed in the following chapter:

These poems are characterized by simpler meanings and more complex auditory patterns than can be found in the early poetry. The structure is more flexible, the rhythm more flowing, and the verbal and visual patterning more complex yet more pervasive. The influence upon Thomas of oral reading accounts in large part for the differences between the early and late poetry. His first extensive oral reading of poetry was during the second world war, when he was on the staff of the B.B.C.[1] As Roy Campbell said, Thomas's discovery that he could read poetry on the radio transformed his later poems for the better.[2] As a result of this discovery — which was reinforced by his public readings in England and, on four different visits, in the United States — Thomas projected

---

[1]   Roy Campbell says that "Dylan was the best all-round reader of verse that I ever produced ... [though] he was best at the 'wild and wooly' poets". ("Memories of Dylan Thomas at the B.B.C.", *Poetry*, LXXXVII [November, 1955], p. 112.)

[2]   Referred to by Herbert Marshall McLuhan, "Sight, Sound, and the Fury", *Commonweal*, IX (April 9, 1954), p. 7.

into his later poetry some of the dynamic, lyrical qualities of his own rich, resonant voice. Equally important, from his new relationship with the public he was forced to recognize the need for simplification of meaning in any poetry which a person is to understand and appreciate upon first *hearing* rather than *seeing*. Such poetry is more effective, too, if the meaning is universalized rather than merely personalized. And sound, he realized, should assist rather than dominate the sense in poetry of high excellence. At a conference with students at the University of Utah in 1952, Thomas indicated clearly that his new approach was toward simplification and lyricism and that this redirection was inextricably related to his oral reading:

At first I thought it enough to have an impression of sound and feeling and let the meaning seep in later, but since I've been giving these broadcasts and reading other men's poetry as well as my own, I find it better to have more meaning at first reading.

It appears, then, that Thomas's progress toward simplicity and lyricism was to some extent a conscious effort. Through oral reading of poetry on the radio and in lectures, Thomas came to realize that sound and sense should correlate and should simultaneously affect the reader.

XXIII

Thomas originally intended that "In Country Sleep", "Over Sir John's hill", and "In the white giant's thigh" should someday form separate parts of a long poem. In 1950 he said of the projected poem that "some [of it] ... is written down on paper, some of it is in a rough draft in the head, and the rest of it radiantly unworded in ambitious conjecture". This "poem in preparation" was to be on a "grand and simple" plan and was to be called "In Country Heaven". The three separate poems are, unfortunately, the only extant completed portions of the long poem and can give no accurate idea of the form and content it might have had. "I do not yet know myself", Thomas further commented, "their relevance to the whole, hypothetical structure. But I do know they belong to it."[3] Thus it seems valid to treat the three poems almost as separate works in respect to their sound and sense.

The first section of "In Country Sleep" contains nine stanzas of seven lines each, and the second section, eight stanzas of six lines each. The pattern of total number of syllables varies from eleven to fourteen syllables in the long lines, but is always four syllables in the short lines, i.e., line 5 of part 1 and line 4 of part 2. Most of the lines have either five or six strong speech stresses, and there is some variation that correlates with the emotional impact of the particular line. For instance, the following two lines differ greatly in their rhythmic impression and their number of speech stresses. On the one hand, "Sleep, good, for ever slow and deep, spelled rare and wise" (part 1, stanza II), with its many consecutive, heavily stressed monosyllables, is slow and lingering in effect. On the other hand, "Night and the reindeer on the clouds above the haycocks" (part 2, stanza I), with one more syllable but only half as many speech stresses, is quick and light in effect.

It is the taut rhyme scheme which most formally organizes the structure of the poem. The rhyme scheme for part 1 is *abcbaac* and for part 2, *abbcca*. All except five of the fifty-one rhyme-word patterns are masculine. Few of the rhymes are approximate and almost half of the stanzas have two of the three rhymes identical in vowel sound, as in the repetition of the *i* sound in part 1, stanza I:

near, dear, year
asleep, leap
hood, wood.

Moreover, seven different rhyme-bases which appear in the first six stanzas recur later in the poem. In part 1, stanza I, for example, the "near" rhyme is used in stanza IV and again in stanza VIII, the "asleep" rhyme is used in stanza III, and the "hood" rhyme is used in stanza V. Both the assonance-link *within* many of the rhymes of the stanzas and the rhyme-link *between* many of the stanzas contribute to the interlocking nature of the structure of the poem.

"In Country Sleep" abounds in internal rhymes, many of them adjacent to each other or rhyming with the line-end words. These internal rhymes include:

[3] *Quite Early One Morning* (Norfolk, Conn., 1954), p. 180.

Part 1		Part 2	
Stanza		Stanza	
I	near, Fear, dear, dear, year asleep, sheepwhite, leap	I	fair, prayer, there, harecocks, fox
II	Sleep, deep hobnail tales	II	
III	sleep, keep	III	tale, pail
IV	Bell, spell fear, near, clear ride wide dell, well, cell	IV	black-backed
V	tree, three telling, knelling fables, lord's-table	V	blue, true, dew
VI	gay may	VI	
VII	spelled at rest, held and blessed	VII	tide, riding vast night, last night
VII – VIII	seek, meek	VIII	grieve, believe fear, dear, dear
IX	falls, stalls, falls, falls, falls hail, vale		

Several of the internal rhyme-word patterns, such as the "fear" rhyme and the "sleep" rhyme, recur as line-end rhymes. Notice that these two words themselves emphasize ideas basic to the theme of the poem — that is, the father's *fear* that his daughter may not be protected in life as she is in *sleep*.

Although well-defined as to their arrangement of lines, syllables, and rhymes, the stanzas are seldom end-stopped and thus are relatively rapid, fluid in movement. The various parts of the poem are related frequently by repetition and echoes of phrases. Several examples may be cited: "Never and never, my girl" (part 1, stanza I) and "Never, my girl" (part 1, stanza III); "you are shielded by fern / and flower" (part 1, stanza III) and "Be shielded by chant and flower" (part 1, stanza VI); "This night and each vast night", "This night and each night" (part 1, stanza VIII); "The leaping saga of prayer!" (part 2, stanza I), "But her faith that each vast night and the saga of prayer" (part 2, stanza VII); "Her faith that this last night" (part 2, stanza VII), "this night he comes and night without end", "this dawn and each first dawn" (part 2, stanza VIII). Other echoes are fainter and further apart, like "Night and the reindeer" (part 2, stanza I) and "Night and the vein of birds" (part 2, stanza II) or "sly as snow" (part 1, stanza VIII) and "Slyly, slowly" (part 2, stanza VI). Yet all the repetitions and echoes seem to contribute to a chanting effect which characterizes the poet's plea for protection for his child.

Of the numerous and extensive patterns of assonance and consonance in the poem only a few of the most interesting can be pointed out. For instance, sometimes — as in the numerous *i* sounds of part 1, stanza I — the assonance reinforces the vowel sound of the predominant end-rhyme. Sometimes words in identical vertical positions of adjacent lines are subtly and intricately related. Part 1, stanza II, lines 1 and 2 conclude, respectively, with the phrases "rare and wise" and "rose and shire". "Rare" and "rose" are linked by alliteration, "wise" and "shire" by assonance, "rare" and "shire" by final consonance, "wise" and "rose" by final consonance.

Other varieties of lattice-work in sound are also skillfully unobtrusive, but help to create the general impression of a harmony which can lull the poet's little girl to sleep. In part 1, stanza III, for example, the phrase "until tolled to sleep" is interlocked by the initial and final consonance in "-til" and "tolled". In the following stanza the end-rhyme and internal rhyme of "Bell" and "spell" and later of "dell", "well", and "cell" is twice softly echoed in the lyrical statement, "A hill touches an angel". In part 1, stanza II, the consonance of *t* and *l* sounds binds together the words "tolls", "stall", and "tales". Cross-alliteration of the voiced continuants *l* and *m* is evident in the relationship between the phrases "Illumination of music!" and "Music of elements", which are placed in initial positions in lines 1 and 5, respectively, of part 1, stanza IV.

In large part the lullaby, lyrical effect of the poetry of "In Country Sleep" results from the extensive use, throughout the poem, of the voiced continuant *l*. Part 1, stanza IX, serves as a good illustration; here the twenty-one occurrences of the sound *l*, including repetitions of the word "fall," retard and punctuate the rhythm. Frequently the *l* sound appears in conjunction with the voiced continuant *s*, as in "spelled asleep". Indeed the emphasis throughout part 1 on the consonants in "spelled asleep" extends the literal meaning associated with these key words of the poem. In part 1 stanza VII, the voiced continuants and the internal rhyme in the first five lines contrast strikingly with the explosives in the final two lines, just as the father's hope for his child's peaceful rest (in the opening lines) contrasts with his fears for her safety (in the closing two lines). The entire poem is a father's prayerful hope that his daughter be protected in life, as in sleep.

XXIV

"Over Sir John's hill" concerns a hawk that kills young birds above the River Towy while a heron and a poet watch. The elegiac nature of the poem makes appropriate its relatively slow, lyrical rhythm. The line lengths of a single stanza vary from one to fourteen or fifteen syllables. A discernible regularity exists, however, in the syllabic count of the respective lines of the five stanzas. As Ralph N. Maud notes, the work sheets of "Over Sir John's hill" reveal that Thomas counted syllables at a certain stage in developing the poem, but later abandoned absolute regularity of syllabic count in order to include certain phrases.[4] The result is:

Stanza	Number of Syllables in Each Line
I	5 6 14 15 5 1 15 5 14 5 14 14
II	5 6 13 14 5 1 13 6 13 4 13 14
III	5 6 13 14 4 1 14 4 15 5 14 13
IV	5 6 14 14 5 1 14 4 14 4 13 13
V	5 6 14 14 6 1 13 5 14 6 14 13

A notable phenomenon in "Over Sir John's hill" is the almost

---

[4] See "Language and Meaning in the Poetry of Dylan Thomas". Unpublished Ph. D. dissertation, Harvard University (1958), pp. 152-153.

complete avoidance of polysyllables and the very emphatic nature
of closely juxtaposed monosyllables, which are reinforced by all
kinds of phonetic echoes, sometimes so crowded as to make
enunciation difficult unless one reads the poem slowly. This
parading of emphatic monosyllabism culminates in the one-syllable
links in the middle of each stanza. Each one-syllable line appears
as a pivot around which the stanza turns. Before the pivot the
flow seems to be narrowing and slowing down, whereas after it the
flow seems to be expanding and accelerating. In particular, the
long line after the monosyllabic one usually has a number of disyl-
labic words — in stanza II there is even one of four syllables
("elegiac") — which quicken and smooth the pace. Thus the total
rhythmic pattern in each stanza is one of contraction and ex-
pansion.

In the relationships between the end-words of the lines, "Over
Sir John's hill" is complex. The comments made by Gilbert Highet
concerning the rhyme scheme of the poem are somewhat over-
simplified,[5] for the relationships between the line-end words run
the gamut from full-rhyme to varieties of consonantal and assonantal similarities.

Stanza	End-Word	Line
I	hill, still, until	1, 2, 9
	claws, Wars	3, 6
	bay, play	4, 5
	hedges, heron, headstone	7, 11, 12
	squawk, hawk	8, 10
II	crack, jack-, hawk	1, 2, 9
	hare, There	3, 6
	fins, wind	4, 5
	paddles, passage, prancing	7, 11, 12
	dab-filled, killed	8, 10
III	shell, bell, elm	1, 2, 9

[5] In saying that "The seventh and ninth lines have no corresponding rhymes",
Highet overlooks the relationships which the end-words of these lines usually
bear to, respectively, the eleventh and twelfth lines, and the first and second
lines. ("The Great Welsh Poet: Dylan Thomas", excerpt from *The Powers
of Poetry*, in *Vogue*, CXXXV [March 15, 1960], p. 152.)

	sung, Young	3, 6
	brand, shall	4, 5
	dilly, dingle, distant	7, 11, 12
	die, I	8, 10
IV	vale, sail hail	1, 2, 9
	stilt, Guilt	3, 6
	elmed, knelled	4, 5
	whistles, windows, whispering	7, 11, 12
	on, song	8, 10
V	go, snow, slow	1, 2, 9
	owl, Shout	3, 6
	elms, hens	4, 5
	scaly, shaken, sailing	7, 11, 12
	waves, graves	8, 10

Close observation of these sets of end-words reveals a distinct progression from a predominance of full-rhyme in the first stanza ("hill", "still", "until"; "bay", "play"; "squawk", "hawk") to a predominance of assonance in the final stanza ("owl", "Shout"; "elms", "hens"; "scaly", "waves", "grave", "shaken", "sailing"). Yet, interestingly enough, the *scheme* for the relationship between the end-words is the same in all stanzas — *aabccbdeaedd* — no matter whether the relationship itself is mainly that of full-rhyme, consonance, or assonance. In stanza V assonance of the same vowel occurs in lines 7, 8, 10, 11, and 12, but the line-end words in 7, 11, and 12 are more closely linked with each other — through similar initial consonants — than with the line-end words in lines 8 and 10.

A number of line-end words in "Over Sir John's hill" rhyme with words within the line. In stanza I, "shrill" (line 5) rhymes with "hill" and "still", and "rays" (line 4) echoes "bay" and "play". In stanza II, "black" (line 2) rhymes with "crack" and "jack-" in the lines

> Flash, and the plumes crack,
> And a black cap of jack-
>
> . . . .

The proximity of these three rhymes, the assonance linking them with two of the three other stressed syllables of the lines ("Flash" and "cap"), the punctuation marks (including the hyphenation of an endword), and the predominance of explosives (p, b, and k), all tend to create a forceful and staccato tempo which reinforces the sense of these lines.

Internal rhyme and approximate rhyme are relatively frequent throughout the poem, as in "slowly" and "holy" (stanza I, line 11), "There / Where" (stanza II, lines 6 and 7), "stabs" and "dab-" (stanza II, lines 7 and 8), "paddles" and "pebbly" (stanza III, lines 7 and 8), "'dilly dilly'" (stanza II, line 9 and stanza III, line 7), "grieve" and "leave" (stanza III, line 9), and "hoot" and "looted" (stanza V, lines 3 and 4). Alliteration pervades the poem and is especially effective when used subtly, as in the case of the cross-alliterated pairs of words, "Shallow and sedge" and "psalms and shadows" (stanza II, lines 9 and 12). Consonance and assonance are skillfully interwoven in numerous instances. In the phrase "Sir John's elmed / Hill, telltale the knelled / Guilt", the frequency of the vowels ε and ι and of the voiced continuant l emphasizes the key phrase "knelled / Guilt", and the juxtaposition of the final d of "knelled" and the initial g of "Guilt" forces a slow reading of the passage.

In the concluding stanza the poet comments on the natural sounds which he hears on Sir John's hill; these sounds remind him of the once-familiar sounds of the young birds now dead. The staccato rhythms of the explosives in these opening lines (e.g., "snapt", "cupt", and "Shout") echo the sense, the sharp sounds of the hoot owl and the blown grassblade. By contrast, the conclusion is the more effective, for its long vowels (o and e) and voiced consonants (s and l) reinforce the solemn and slow music of the elegy. That is, in the closing line the poet laments not simply the death of young birds but mortality itself, when he grieves "for the sake of the souls of the slain birds sailing".

XXV

"In the white giant's thigh" is a romantic poem in which long dead women, who in life were childless, reveal to the poet their longing, even in death, to bear children. Although "In the white giant's thigh" contains ambiguous, erotic imagery — such as the "white giant's thigh", which is a Welsh landmark as well as a sexual image — it is actually as devoid of bawdry as "Lament" is full of it. The beauty of the poem lies chiefly in "the general feel and sound of it", as Thomas expressed it.[6]

The complex verbal and visual patterning of "In the white giant's thigh" is relatively unobtrusive. Although the rhyme scheme falls neatly into the *abab* pattern repeated fifteen times, with each of the thirty rhymes except two a full rhyme and each of the sixty rhyme words except five a monosyllable, yet the obviousness of this scheme is disguised, since the poem consists of paragraphs of various lengths, rather than regular quatrain stanzas; since less than half the lines are retarded by any punctuation mark, a fact which lessens the emphasis on the rhymes; and since the same rhyme words almost never recur.[7]

In the first portion of the poem the paragraphs are shorter than in the last portion, and the early, short paragraphs seem particularly cohesive because of the internal rhyme, which appears seldom in the later, longer paragraphs. Internal rhymes flow thickly in the opening lines of the poem: "high" and "lie" with line-end rhymes "cry" and "thigh"; "night", "white"; "there", "Where"; "though", "ago"; "they lay" and "bay" with line-end rhymes "pray" and "away"; "Pleading", "seed", "weed"; "Though" with line-end rhymes "ago" and "flow".

Many of the poetic devices utilized in the first portion of the poem seem concentrated in the description of the long-ago love scenes of the passionate, dead country women,

> ... Who once in gooseskin winter loved all ice leaved
> In the courters' lanes, or twined in the ox roasting sun
> In the wains tonned so high that the wisps of the hay
> Clung to the pitching clouds, or gay with any one
> Young as they in the after milking moonlight lay.

---

[6] *Quite Early One Morning*, p. 183.
[7] The notable exception is the rhyme words "hill" and "still", which occur both at the beginning and end of the poem. The repetition serves to stress the importance of the meaning of these words to the poem as a whole.

The lushness of the lines evokes the sense of physical longing which
is expressed in terms of the creative urge of nature. Internal full or
approximate rhymes occur in "gooseskin winter"; "lanes", "wains";
"sun", "tonned"; "Clung", "Young"; "gay", "they" (linked with
the line-end rhymes "hay", "lay"). Alliteration of the voiced continuants *l* and *m* in "milking moonlight lay" produces a restful and
smooth effect which is in keeping with the sensual meaning. A
more intricate relationship occurs in the phrase "loved all ice
leaved", in which "loved" and "leaved" are identical in initial and
final consonants and the voiced continuant *l* is echoed in the inter-
vening word "all".

Two consecutive lines, forming a single paragraph, offer a
striking contrast in sound effects:

> Or rippling soft in the spinney moon as the silk
> And ducked and draked white lake that harps to a hail stone.

The lines continue the recollection of the women's love-making by
describing the flesh quivering in the act of love like a lake that
ripples in response to a hailstone. The smooth, voiced continuants
(*s*, *r*, *l*, *m*, and *n*) and the repetition of the short vowel *i* in the
first line contrast with the explosives (predominantly the consonants
d, *k*, and *t*) and the repetition of the long vowel *e* in the second line.
The stress patterns further contribute to the emotional impact of the
lines. Beginning similarly with two iambs, the lines then differ
sharply in stress pattern: to help create the legato effect of the first
line, unstressed syllables occur more frequently than stressed
syllables; to help create the staccato effect of the second line, consecutive stressed monosyllables occur in "draked white lake" and
"hail stone". Within the context, these two lines are superb examples of correlation of sound and sense.

In other passages, too, sound reflects sense. The tumbling rhythm
and clipped explosives of "butter fat goosegirls, bounced in a gambo
bed" reinforce the sense. It is perhaps noteworthy that the word
"gambo", which denotes a simple farm cart, has special connotations in this context. Since the word "goose" occurs near the word
"gambo", there is a verbal association with the gambo goose, an
African spur-winged goose; more significantly, there is a verbal

association between "gambo" and "gambol", a skipping or leaping about in frolic, which reinforces the literal meaning of the bouncing girls in the cart. A second interesting passage concerns the barrenness of the women, who

> ... nothing bore, no mouthing babe to the veined hives
> Hugged, and barren and bare on Mother Goose's ground.

Here the words "bore, no", "barren", and "bare on" all hollowly echo each other and enhance the sense.

Although in life the women's love bore no fruit, in death their love can be influential. The poet pleads that the women will

> Teach me the love that is evergreen after the fall leaved
> Grave, after Beloved on the grass gulfed cross is scrubbed
> Off by the sun.

The first line here is smooth and flowing, with repetition of the stressed *i* vowel ("Teach", "green", "leaved") and of continuants (*l* and *r*). In contrast is the more forceful and dynamic phrase in the second line, which uses different arrangements of similar explosives (*g* and *k*) — usually in combination with the continuant *r* — "*gr*ass gulfed *cr*oss is *scr*ubbed". And within these women, the poet says, love lives on, "Love for ever meridian". The concluding line symbolizes this all-consuming yet deathless love:

> And the daughters of darkness flame like Fawkes fires still.

This flaring image alludes to the country custom of lighting bonfires on each November 5, Guy Fawkes Day. Thomas, who considered Thomas Hardy his favorite twentieth-century poet, may even have associated the lines with the dark and passionate Eustacia Vye who, in a climactic early chapter of *The Return of the Native*, uses her "Fawkes fire" as a signal for her lover, Damon Wildeve. Certainly the consonance of *d*, *f*, and *l*, and the repetition of the *s* sibilant, which suggests the hissing flames of bonfires, help create a haunting line. The tempo, beginning relatively swiftly with two anapests, concludes with slowness and finality, on three consecutive stressed monosyllables.

XXVI

"Do not go gentle into that good night" is perhaps too often considered lightly as only simple iteration. Cid Corman even believes
that "the set form of the villanelle treads Thomas's feet".[8] By
definition the villanelle *is* restrictive, because it demands nineteen
lines on two rhymes in six stanzas, the first and third lines of the
opening tercet recurring alternately at the end of the other tercets,
both being repeated at the end of the concluding quatrain. Within this
structure, however, Thomas creates a poem of great force, beauty,
and tenderness, in which sound and sense are exquisitely blended.

Thomas's villanelle is a plea to his ill and aging father to die as
wise men, good men, wild men, grave men die and as the father
himself has lived — struggling, "[raging] against the dying of the
light". The structure of the poem involves two uses of the repeated
lines with some functional change. In the opening stanza, "Do not
go gentle into that good night" and "Rage, rage against the dying
of the light" are imperatives directed to an unidentified person.
In the next four stanzas one or the other of these repeated phrases
forms the predicate to statements about, respectively, wise men,
good men, wild men, and grave men. In the concluding stanza, the
poet directly addresses his father, and the repeated lines thus
become significant imperatives — first the negative command to his
father, "Do not go gentle into that good night"; then the positive
command to him to assert his individuality, "Rage, rage against the
dying of the light".

Numerous other devices contribute to the subtle variations
within the pattern of the villanelle. Although the meter is generally
iambic pentameter and the vocabulary contains seven times as
many monosyllables as polysyllables, the speech stresses in a line
vary from five (the "Rage, rage" line) to eight (the "Do not go
gentle" line) and help save the poem from a monotonous, "sing-
song" rhythm. The full, resonant effect of the poem is intensified
by the fact that the two rhyme-bases involve long vowels (*e* and *ai*).
Especially in stanzas III and V, the rhymes are emphasized by a
concentration of internal assonance of *e* and *ai*:

[8] "Dylan Thomas: Rhetorician in Mid-Career", *Accent*, XIII (Winter, 1953),
p. 58.

Good men, the last wave by, crying how bright
Their frail deeds might have danced in a green bay,
Rage, rage against the dying of the light.
Grave men, near death, who see with blinding sight
Blind eyes could blaze like meteors and be gay,
Rage, rage against the dying of the light.

Both stanzas have at least four uses of each of the rhyme vowels, excluding the rhyme words themselves. The repetition of vowel sounds focuses attention upon the meaningful words of these stanzas; it helps to indicate an important theme underlying the poem — the discrepancy between what the good and grave men have done in life (frail deeds) and what they *might* have done (blazing, meteoric deeds).

Part of the powerfulness of the poem results from the intensity of striking power of the words used. One out of every eight syllables is of very high striking power (ten syllables have a striking power of 39, thirteen have a striking power of 40 to 44). Thus Thomas's language is exhortative in both sound and sense; the words rage as he desires his father to rage.

In the final stanza lies the core of the meaning of the poem. More quiet, calm, and tender than the preceding lines, this stanza directly addresses the poet's father on his precipice of death — i.e., "on the sad height". Then in the second line Thomas urges his father to

Curse, bless, me now with your fierce tears, I pray.

This line of ten monosyllables is strong, deliberate, and slow in tempo. Closely juxtaposed repetitions of the same sound usually produce an effect of retarding the rhythm. Such is the case here, where the s sound, introduced by the word "sad" in the first line of the stanza, is repeated. The three most important words end in the sound s — "curse", "bless", and "fierce" — and "tears" ends in the closely related z sound. Thomas's use of punctuation also retards the rhythm, in particular the non-grammatical use in "curse, bless, me now". Indeed, the oxymoron effect of "curse, bless" reflects the dichotomy and poignancy of Thomas's plea to his father. The poet prays that his father will, with fierce tears, curse and bless him — as his final and ultimate protest against death.

XXVII

In "Lament" an unrepentant old sinner recalls the sensual pleasures of his adolescence, manhood, and prime (in stanzas I, II, and III, respectively) and laments the physical deterioration of his old age and "all the deadly virtues" that attend his deathbed hours (in stanzas IV and V, respectively).

Structurally, "Lament" consists of five stanzas of twelve lines each. The total number of syllables in each line is always either nine or ten:

Stanza	Number of Syllables in Each Line											
I	10	9	10	10	9	10	9	9	10	10	9	9
II	10	9	10	9	10	10	9	10	10	10	9	9
III	10	9	10	9	9	10	10	9	9	9	9	9
IV	10	9	10	9	9	9	9	9	9	9	10	9
V	9	10	10	9	10	9	10	9	10	9	9	10

The number of speech-stressed syllables in each line, however, varies from three to seven.

Various sound patterns in "Lament" correspond generally with the sense of the poem. The first three stanzas, which concern the narrator's wild, lusty past existence, mark a general contrast with the last two stanzas, which concern his subdued, impotent present existence. Two elements of sound which reinforce sense might be discussed in this connection: the contrast in types of consonants and the contrast in metrical patterns. First, many of the consonants in the opening stanzas are explosives. Especially effective clusters of explosives occur in

> Not a boy and a bit in the wick-
> Dipping moon and drunk as a new dropped calf

and in

> Brandy and ripe in my bright, bass prime,
> No springtailed tom in the red hot town.

In the second example, the cognate alliteration of the *p-b* explosives and the assonance of *ai* link closely the words "*Br*andy", "*br*ight", "*pri*me", and "*sp*ring-". In the last stanza, continuants seem more significant than explosives, as in "Now I am a man no more no more". Secondly, in the first four stanzas of the poem a great variety of metrical patterns appears, and the same pattern scarcely ever recurs in the same stanza. At the close of "Lament", however, more regular metrical patterns (to be analyzed later) occur. It seems fitting that metrical irregularity should characterize the opening passages of the poem, which concern the narrator's former irregular and uncontrolled life and that metrical regularity should characterize the passages which concern his present, more regular and controlled life.

As to the rhyme scheme of "Lament", six rhymes occur, in the pattern *abcdabcdefef*. Off-rhyme, usually in the form of final consonance without assonance, is rather equally distributed throughout the stanzas. In stanza V, a complicated rhyme relationship occurs between lines 1 (with its line-end word "more"), 5 (with its line-end words "bells jaw") and 7 (with its line-end words "bore angels"). For "more" "bore" and "bells", "angels" form rhymes. Internal rhyme occurs in several other instances, among the most notable being "blind", "rind", "find" (stanza IV) and "more", "roaring", "bore" (stanza V).

"Lament" utilizes incremental repetition of phrases in the first three lines of each of the five stanzas. In the first line, the phrase "When I was a ..." is repeated in four stanzas, with variations to designate the narrator's youth, manhood, prime, and middle age. Stanza V advances the phrase to the present — "Now I am a..." — to designate the narrator's old age. In the second line the phrase "And the black ... of the ..." occurs in stanzas I, II, and III, and, with substitutions, in stanzas IV and V. The third line offers the fullest incremental repetition: "(Sighed the old ram rod, dying of ...)". Stanza I completes this line with "women", stanza II with "bitches", stanza III with "welcome", stanza IV with "downfall", and stanza V with "strangers". The repetitions of these three lines throughout the poem give structural unity to the piece, and the variations throughout the poem advance or deepen its meaning.

"Lament" follows a general ballad style in both its heavily accented and alliterated verse and in its incremental repetitions. As previously mentioned, the number of speech-stressed syllables in the lines varies greatly as compared with the total number of syllables in the lines. For the most part, these heavy stresses fall toward the end of the line; in seventeen lines three or more consecutively stressed syllables conclude the line. Perhaps the most arresting of these is the line "Oh, time enough when the blood creeps cold", where the use of monosyllables, explosives, and consecutively stressed syllables forces a slow tempo which enhances the literal meaning of the slow flow of blood in the old and dying. The metrical irregularities in the early stanzas only accentuate the strong metrical regularities in the concluding lines (8-12) of the final stanza of the poem:

> Harpies around me out of her womb!
> Chastity prays for me, piety sings,
> Innocence sweetens my last black breath,
> Modesty hides my thighs in her wings,
> And all the deadly virtues plague my death!

Here lines 8, 9, 10, and 11 are identical in the metrical pattern of the first five syllables (a trochee followed by an amphibrach); indeed, lines 8 and 11 are throughout identical metrically. Line 9, except for the addition of a final stressed syllable, is dactylic, and line 12 is completely iambic. Thus the ending provides a fitting climax for the correlation between sound and sense in "Lament", for in the concluding line, expressing the old man's resignation — unwilling though it may be — to death, the rhythmic pattern yields to complete regularity and flowing smoothness.

XXVIII

"Poem on his Birthday", the last of Thomas's three birthday poems, first appeared in October, 1951, in *World Review* (New Series). This early version consisted of only nine stanzas of nine lines each. Later Thomas revised the poem, adding three new stanzas, and in this form it appeared in *In Country Sleep* and ultimately in the *Collected Poems*.

In structure "Poem on his Birthday" is extremely elaborate. The twelve stanzas contain nine lines each. As in "Lament", the verse is rather strictly patterned in regard to the number of syllables in each line, but the arrangement of speech-stressed syllables is quite irregular. The odd-numbered lines have six syllables and the even-numbered lines, nine syllables. There are only two departures from this arrangement — stanza I, line 9, which lacks one syllable, and stanza XI, line 5, which contains an extra syllable:

Stanza	Number of Syllables in Each Line
I	6 9 6 9 6 9 6 9 5
II	6 9 6 9 6 9 6 9 6
III	6 9 6 9 6 9 6 9 6
IV	6 9 6 9 6 9 6 9 6
V	6 9 6 9 6 9 6 9 6
VI	6 9 6 9 6 9 6 9 6
VII	6 9 6 9 6 9 6 9 6
VIII	6 9 6 9 6 9 6 9 6
IX	6 9 6 9 6 9 6 9 6
X	6 9 6 9 6 9 6 9 6
XI	6 9 6 9 7 9 6 9 6
XII	6 9 6 9 6 9 6 9 6

In contrast to this regularity, the number of speech-stressed syllables in each line varies, in no eatablished pattern, from two to seven.

"Poem on his Birthday" uses no rigid rhyme scheme, but, in addition to scattered initial consonance and final consonance in the line-end words, assonance occurs in a definite pattern, *ababcdcdc*:

Stanza		Stanza	
I	sun, scud	III	fall, hawks
	sea, beaks		fly, glide
	birds, spurns, spear		drowned, house, shroud
	grave, age		He, perceives
II	go, told	IV	robe, knows
	trails, waves		prayer, end
	death, bell, bless		cloud, down, mouth
	room, wounds		dust, blood

V swung, struck	IX old, foam
knells, wrecked	wild, shrined
stars, apart, dark	vows, aground, aloud
cage, flame	run, tongue
VI lost	X five, slime
great, place	love, come
God, was	domes, bones, most
true, woods	selves, flesh
void, joy	
VII bare, dead	XI move, blooms
bay, whales	hulks, exults
geese, priest, peace	way, faith, praise
ghost, fold	then, said
VIII way, prays	XII hills, sing
alone, blow	brown, how
hills, kick, Him	ride, eyes, die
last, stars	Oh, alone

Exceptions occur in the *c* rhyme of stanza I, in the *b* rhyme of stanza IV, in the *a* rhyme of stanza VII, and throughout stanza VI. And the overall pattern of assonance in the line-end words is unobtrusive and intricate.

Like most of Thomas's late poems, "Poem on his Birthday" is studded with internal full-rhymes or approximate rhymes. In many instances, one of the linked words is a line-end word: "cold", "told" (II, 2, 3); "Waves", "ways" (II, 4, 5); "fly", "sky" (III, 2, 4); "drowned", "towns" (III, 5, 6); "knells", "bells", "skull" (V, 2, 3, 4); "aground", "tumbledown" (IX, 7, 8); "kingdom come" (X, 4); "I", "die" (XII, 9).

In part the slow, lyrical effect of "Poem on his Birthday" results from the general absence of sustained clusters of consonants and from the frequency of words which begin or end in vowel sounds. Several examples might be cited, such as

> *A*nd far *a*t *se*a *he* knows,
> Wh*o* slaves t*o* his crouched, *e*ternal *e*nd
> *U*nder *a* serpent cloud
>
> . . . .

or

Dark *is a way a*nd light *is a* place,
Heaven that never was
Nor will b*e ev*er *is a*lways tr*ue*

. . . .

or

But dark *is a* long w*ay*,
H*e*, on the *earth of* the night, *a*lone
With *a*ll th*e* living, prays.

As in much of Thomas's most lyrical poetry, the ingenious use of
explosives and continuants is highly effective. Perhaps the most
illuminating passage in this respect in "Poem on his Birthday" is
the stanza describing the poet's ultimate and final blessing,

That the closer I move
To death, one man through his sundered hulks,
The louder the sun blooms
And the tusked, ramshackling sea exults;
And every wave of the way
And gale I tackle, the whole world then,
With more triumphant faith
Than ever was since the world was said,
Spins its morning of praise.

In the opening lines of this passage continuants dominate most
of the semantically important words. In the later lines clipped,
pulsating explosives suggest the meaning of a vibrant, triumphant
life force, as in line 4, "And the tusked, ramshackling sea exults".
Assonance pervades the stanza, for the middle vowel ʌ occurs in
"*o*ne", "s*u*ndered", "h*u*lks", "s*u*n", "t*u*sked", "ex*u*lts", and the
high vowel *e* occurs in "w*a*ve", "w*a*y", "g*a*le", and "f*ai*th".
Internal full rhyme and approximate rhyme occur occasionally,
as in "one", "sun", and "ramshackling", "tackle". Such phonetic
devices help create the beauty of stanza XI.

Yet the unified effect of the eleventh stanza stems largely from
its total organization. In the stanza the odd-numbered lines are
shorter (usually containing two anapests or three iambs), and the
even-numbered lines are longer (usually containing four recognizable
metrical stresses). Except for the addition of a short line at the
beginning, the stanza organization here — and throughout "Poem

on his Birthday" — approaches that of the ballad stanza. The
alternation between short and long lines produces a smooth cadence,
partially because the shorter lines are run-on. Stanza XI is, moreover, only a section of a long poetic statement whose effect is that
of one continuous, powerful crescendo. The meter accentuates the
crescendo in that most lines begin smoothly and swiftly with an
unstressed and semantically unimportant word, till the surging
ninth line opens emphatically with an important, stressed expression: "Spins its morning of praise."

Following the climactic eleventh stanza, the conclusion subsides
into comparative simplicity and calm. In the final lines the assonance of the dark vowel *o* and of the diphthong *ai* dominate the
melodic element:

> More spanned with angels ride
> The mansouled fiery islands! Oh,
> Holier then their eyes,
> And my shining men no more alone
> As I sail out to die.

CONCLUSION

In the light of the preceding chapters, it is apparent that Thomas developed in auditory techniques from the staccato nature of the early poetry to the legato nature of the later poetry. He achieved an orchestration in three general ways: (1) by his arrangement of stresses; (2) by his choice of sounds; (3) by his arrangement of sounds.

In its arrangement of stresses, Thomas's poetry reveals a progression from a poetry of rather strong metrical stress, to a poetry of flowing cadence. In the early poetry the metrical pattern is relatively regular; "From love's first fever to her plague", "The hand that signed the paper", "Should lanterns shine", and "When all my five and country senses see" (for example) all tend toward an iambic pattern. Other factors also contribute to the strongly stressed rhythm in the early poems — the widespread use of words with high striking power, of monosyllables, and of end-stopped lines. In the later poetry the patterns of metrical stress are more diverse and irregular. In general, the ratio of stressed to unstressed words is smaller than in the early period. Further, the structure of the later poems is more fluid, especially in that the lines — and frequently the paragraphs or stanzas themselves — are run-on.

In the choice of sounds, Thomas's poetry reveals a distinct progression toward a phonetic "symbolism". To varying degrees the sound echoes the sense in his poetry. In the early period sound usually enhances sense only in a phrase or line. In a poem of the middle period, frequently two sections which contrast in sense will also contrast in predominant sounds. For instance, in "'If my head hurt a hair's foot'" the child's speech is characterized primarily by explosives, the mother's speech, primarily by continuants; in "Once below a time" the description of the immature poet is characterized primarily by explosives, the description of the mature poet, primarily by continuants. In the late poetry, sound and sense are more frequently integrated; passages in which sound echoes sense are often sustained. Since Thomas's choice of sounds becomes increasingly selective and increasingly related to the emotional meaning of the poetry and since the tone of his poetry becomes increasingly hymnic and expansive, it is not surprising that the *types* of sounds predominant in Thomas's poetry change. Generally, the early poetry is marked by its frequency of effective consonantal clusters, particularly of explosives (*p, t, k, b, d*, and *g*). In contrast, the later poetry is marked by its frequency of effective vowels, its avoidance of any very continuous use of harsh consonantal clusters, and the prevalence of continuants (especially *s, l, m*, and *r*).

Thomas's poetic development is, however, more pronounced in the arrangement of sounds than in the arrangement of stresses or even in the choice of sounds. Many early poems resort to glaring repetitions, such as phrasal or syntactical repetitions which fail to broaden or deepen significantly the total meaning of the poem, like the repetitions based on the phrase "where no sun shines" in "Light breaks where no sun shines", or even sometimes mere "self-plagiarism", like the repetition of certain vague words, only seldom justified. Gradually, however, the arrangements of sound become more subtle, varied, and pervasive. The complex and diffused auditory patterns in these later poems prove that assonance, alliteration, full and approximate rhyme (both internally and at line-end) form the basis of Thomas's distinctive instrumentation. Thomas strived consciously for unobtrusive yet rich verbal effects and came to distrust obvious and easy sound patterns. Speaking of rhyme words, Thomas once commented, "Rhymes are coming to me naturally, too, which I distrust; I like looking for connections, not finding them tabulated in stations".[1] Such a preoccupation with words is understandable. From an early age, Thomas was interested in "the shapes of sounds", as Daniel Jones, his boyhood

[1]   *LVW*, p. 36.

companion substantiates in his accounts of their games of "serious play" involving collaboration in prose and poetry.[2] And in the later poetry it is as if Thomas were dealing in verbal alchemy, so complex and effective are the auditory patterns. "Fern Hill" and "Poem in October" — to mention only two — are radiant lyrics abounding in haunting melodic reverberations. Indeed in most of the later poetry, Thomas's artistic devices reveal greater refinement and his total structure shows greater organic unity than in the early pieces.

Thomas's manipulation of affinitive sound patterns in the late poems is intricate and meaningful; it transcends a merely felicitous combination of words. Thomas's oral reading, on the radio and in poetry lectures, helped him realize the necessity for correlating sound and sense. By his own assertion, his later poetry attempts to achieve simplicity and lyricism by harmonizing sound and sense. Proof that his late poetry is more successful than his early poetry lies in the fact that in the lyrics Thomas *does* often communicate immediately to the listener or reader the synthesis between sound and sense which he tried to achieve. At such a poetic level, sound and sense are inseparable in creating a memorable emotional experience.

Thomas's progression in the relationship in his poetry between sound and sense is, then, quite clear: the early poems are relatively complex and obscure in sense and relatively simple and obvious in auditory patterns; the later poems are relatively simple in sense and relatively complex in auditory patterns. Further, the later poetry — in contrast to the earlier — reveals a more sustained balance between sound and sense.

This book has attempted to illuminate certain aspects of sound and sense in Thomas's poetry. It could not, of course, be definitive or altogether conclusive. Since poetry is an emotional, not a rational, procedure, analysis of some of the subtlest and loveliest auditory effects is impossible. As Thomas said, "You can struggle with rhyme and metre and style and still not have a poem".[3] Yet a

---

[2] See "Dylan Thomas: Memories and Appreciations", *Encounter*, II (January, 1954), pp. 9-10.
[3] Marjorie Adix, "Dylan Thomas: Memories and Appreciations", *Encounter*, II (January, 1954), p. 13.

poem of high excellence necessarily involves auditory techniques, rhythm, and style, and an understanding of these elements at least *contributes* to an appreciation of "moments of magical accident" in poetry.

A THOMAS DISCOGRAPHY

RECORDED READINGS BY DYLAN THOMAS

Title	Date and Place of Recording	Circumstances	Contents[1]
London Library of Recorded English; 4 albums of 6 12-inch records; 78 rpm.; Book I, record 3.			"The War Song of Dinas Vawr", Thomas Love Peacock "The Three Wise Men of Gotham", Thomas Love Peacock
Alpha Records: *Master Recordings in English Litera-*		A repressing of the London Library of Recorded English (*q.v.*)	

[1] All titles refer to works by Dylan Thomas if no other author is mentioned. All titles refer to poetry unless otherwise indicated.

Title	Date and Place of Recording	Circumstances	Contents
ture; 1 12-inch; 33⅓ rpm; Album 1, book 1, side 1, band 8; side 2, band 1.			
Columbia ML 4259:[2] *Pleasure Dome. An Audible Anthology Of Modern Poetry Read by Its Creators;* 1 12-inch; 33⅓ rpm.; Side 2, band 3.	Summer, 1949 London, England (This original tape was probably transferred to a master-record on October 7, 1949, in New York City.)	Lloyd Frankenberg asked Dylan Thomas, in correspondence, if he would consent to record. He agreed. A long time passed — during which all the other poets represented in *Pleasure Dome* were recorded — and Frankenberg and the Columbia Record Company were growing apprehensive; no one in America had ever heard Thomas read and (in respect to his reading) knew only that he had broadcast extensively on BBC. Finally the London office said the tape was made, but it was late September before it arrived in New York City.[3]	"Poem in October" "In my Craft or Sullen Art"

Caedmon TC 1002 Vol I; 1 12-inch; 33⅓ rpm.	February 22, 1952 New York City	Informal afternoon recording. Impromptu selection of readings. Flawless first performance.	"A Child's Christmas in Wales" (story) "Do not go gentle into that good night" "Fern Hill" "In the white giant's thigh" "Ballad of the Long-legged Bait" "Ceremony After a Fire Raid"
Caedmon TC 1018 Vol. II; 1 12-inch; 33⅓ rpm.	June 2, 1953 New York City	Recorded midnight to 4:00 a.m. Selections planned in advance. Imperfect, strained first performance.	"And death shall have no dominion" "Should lanterns shine" "Poem on his birthday" "A Refusal to Mourn the Death, by Fire, of a Child in London" "If I were tickled by the rub of love" "There was a Saviour" "A Winter's Tale" "Lament"
Caedmon TC 1043 Vol. III; 1 12-inch; 33⅓ rpm.	March 7, 1952 Massachusetts Institute of Technology, Boston	The introduction ("A Few Words of a Kind") taped live before an audience at MIT, the poems later recorded in the studio.	"A Few Words of a Kind" (talk) "In Country Sleep" "Over Sir John's hill" "The Hunchback in the Park"

[2] In a letter from Columbia Records, dated July 5, 1961, I was informed that Columbia does not possess any tapes of material read by Dylan Thomas which have not been released.

[3] This information was kindly supplied by Mr. Frankenberg in a letter of September 23, 1961.

Title	Date and Place of Recording	Circumstances	Contents
			"On the Marriage of a Virgin"
			"Light breaks where no sun shines"
			"After the funeral"
Caedmon TC 1061 Vol. IV; 1 12-inch; 33⅓ rpm.	May 11 (?), 1953 Massachusetts Institute of Technology, Boston	"A Visit to America" taped live before an audience at MIT, the poems recorded by Station WGBH, Cambridge.	"A Visit to America" (talk)
			"The Bards", Walter de la Mare
			"Master and Bos'n Song", W. H. Auden
			"As I Walked Out One Evening", W. H. Auden
			"Chard Witlow: Mr. T. S. Eliot's Sunday Evening Broadcast Postscript", Henry Reed
			"Naming of Parts", Henry Reed
			"The Owl", Edward Thomas
			"Broken Appointment", Thomas Hardy
			"To Lisbie Brown", Thomas Hardy
			"In Death Divided", Thomas Hardy
Caedmon TC 1132 Vol. V;⁴ 1 12-inch; 33⅓ rpm.			"Quite Early One Morning" (prose)
			"Reminiscences of Childhood" (prose)
			"A Visit to Grandpa's" (story)
			"Holiday Memory" (prose)

Caedmon TC 2005; May 14, 1953   Dylan Thomas and the original *Under Milk Wood* (a play for voices)
2 12-inch; 33⅓ rpm. Poetry Center of   cast in the premiere performance.

⁴ In a letter of April 20, 1961, I asked the Caedmon publishers whether or not they possess tapes of Thomas's readings which they have not recorded commercially. The publishers acknowledged that they do, but declined answering any questions concerning the contents, date, place, and circumstance of such tapes and whether or not they anticipate releasing further commercial recordings of Thomas's readings.

After this study was completed, Caedmon released (in November, 1963) two 33⅓ rpm. LP records entitled *Dylan Thomas Reading his Complete Recorded Poetry* (TC 2014). The title of the album and the assertion on the inside jacket that "The poems in this album are all of his own that Dylan recorded" are incorrect. The album contains all the poems by Dylan Thomas recorded on Caedmon volumes I, II, and III and on the Columbia *Pleasure Dome*. In addition, it contains seven poems not available previously on a commercial recording:

"Author's Prologue"
"The hand that signed the paper"
"Altarwise by owl-light" (first verse only)
"The tombstone told when she died"
"If my head hurt a hair's foot'"
"Love in the Asylum"
"Among those Killed in the Dawn Raid was a Man Aged a Hundred"

The University of Florida tape includes five poems which the Caedmon *"Complete" Recorded Poetry* does not include:

"From love's first fever to her plague"
"Especially when the October wind"
"It is the sinners' dust-tongued bell"
"Once below a time"
"When all my five and country senses see"

(Cf. footnote 3 to Appendix IV: Thomas's Reading and Recording Itinerary in America.) I am currently attempting to find out, from the sponsors of Thomas's public readings, whether or not other tapes are extant. Perhaps the Caedmon album does contain all the *commercially* or *publicly* taped poems of Thomas reading Thomas, but — if only because it omits the poems taped privately by Gene Baro at the University of Florida — the album is not Dylan Thomas reading his *complete* recorded poetry.

Title	Date and Place of Recording	Circumstances	Contents
	the YM-YWHA at Lexington Avenue and 92nd Street, New York City		"Fern Hill" "A Refusal to Mourn the Death, by Fire, of a Child in London"
Caedmon TC 2006; Caedmon Treasury of Modern Poets; 2 12-inch; 33⅓ rpm.; Side 2, bands 6 and 7	From same original recording as in Vol. I (q.v.) From same original recording as in Vol. II (q.v.)		

RECORDINGS OF THOMAS'S WORK READ BY OTHERS

Title	Date and Place of Recording	Reader	Contents
Argo RG 29; Homage to Dylan Thomas; 1 12-inch; 33⅓ rpm.	1954 Globe Theatre, London (Recorded in collaboration with the Group Theatre)	[Louis MacNeice Hugh Griffith Richard Burton Emlyn Williams Richard Burton	"Requiem Canto", Louis MacNeice] excerpt from "Return Journey" (story) "Poem in October" "A Visit to Grandpa's" (story) "Fern Hill"

Westminster 18076; *Homage to Dylan Thomas*; 1 12-inch; 33⅓ rpm.	[Repressing of Argo tape?]	Richard Burton: Hugh Griffith Emlyn Williams [Louis MacNeice]	"The Hunchback in the Park" "Poem in October" "Fern Hill" excerpt from "Return Journey" (story) "A Visit to Grandpa's" and other prose "Requiem Canto", Louis MacNeice]
Argo RG 21 and 22; 2 12-inch; 33⅓ rpm.	January 25, 1954 London (Recorded with the co-operation of the British Broadcasting Corporation)	Douglas Cleverdon's production of the play, as broadcast. Richard Burton, Hugh Griffith, and the full BBC cast.	*Under Milk Wood* (a play for voices)
Westminster 2202; 2 12-inch; 33⅓ Spoken Arts SA 791-792; 2 12-inch; 33⅓ rpm.	[Repressing of Argo tape?] From same original recording as Argo RG 21 and 22 (*q.v.*)	The British Broadcasting Corporation's production	*Under Milk Wood* (a play for voices)
Argo RG 43; 1 12-inch; 33⅓ rpm.	1955 London	Richard Burton	"In my Craft and Sullen Art" "The force that through the green fuse drives the flower" "A Winter's Tale" "The hand that signed the paper"

Title	Date and Place of Recording	Reader	Contents
Spoken Arts SA 789: *Fifteen Poems by Dylan Thomas*; 1 12-inch; 33⅓ rpm.	From same original recording as Argo RG 43 (*q.v.*)		"Ballad of the Long-legged Bait" "Fern Hill" "The Hunchback in the Park" "Deaths and Entrances" "Before I knocked" "I see the boys of summer" "Lament" "Lie Still, Sleep Becalmed" "Do not go gentle into that good night" "Poem in October" "And death shall have no dominion"
RCA-Victor LM 1883: *Poet's Gold— Verses of Today* (selected by Whit Burnett); 1 12-inch; 33⅓ rpm.		Geraldine Brooks Norman Rose	"Lament" "Do not go gentle into that good night"

APPENDICES

It was an original purpose of this study to analyze the twenty-eight selected poems in respect to three physical elements of sound: striking power, tone, and pitch.

The striking power, the relative intensity or dynamic power, is the capacity of syllables or words to command auditory attention. The calculation for striking power — like that for tone and pitch — was made for each syllable of each poem. The procedure for gauging striking power followed — with some inevitable modifications for British English — the acoustic table of striking power established by the research of Ernest Robson.[1] His table is based upon the striking powers of the individual sounds of speech, which were evaluated in syllables whose tone levels and time durations were constant. The table presents the striking power numbers in numerical positions relative to the weakest sound (*th*), which is assigned the number 1. Thus the striking power numbers of the stronger sounds are solely indications of their striking power as it is relative to the sound *th*. Each articulated vowel or consonant contributes its own striking power to the syllable which contains it. Naturally, the greater the number or density of consonants in a syllable, the greater its striking power.[2]

The tone is the innate "musical" notation of the vowel sounds, based upon the positions of the mouth in articulating the particular vowel. For Thomas's pronunciation, the vowel scale listed below was used. The classification is not a strictly scientific one, but does arrange the vowels in a continuum (from 13 to 1), beginning with those pronounced high and toward the front of the mouth, progressing through those pronounced low to those pronounced high and toward the back of the mouth. In the case of vowels with a muffled quality (ə, ʌ, ɝ, and ɚ) and of diphthongs, their arrangement depends upon the impression they produce on the hearer. The total effect, then, is an arrangement in relative order from clear, thin, bright vowels to darker, richer, more resonant vowels. For present purposes, it is useful to group certain vowels which are similar in the impression they produce on the hearer, although it should be pointed out that technically the sounds are different:

13	i, ɪ, ɪə, e
12	ɛ
11	ae
10	aɪ
9	a
8	ə, ʌ, ɚ, ɝ
7	ɔɪ

---

[1] See *The Orchestra of the Language* (New York, 1959), p. 156 [Table 4].
[2] The account of Robson's method of assessing striking power derives from the explanations in *The Orchestra of the Language*, pp. 43-44.

6 au
5 ɪu
4 ʊ
3 o
2 u
1 ə

The pitch, or relative "musical" notation of the individual speaker's syllables, was estimated by concentrated and repeated listenings to each syllable of the recordings of the twenty-eight poems. The following discussion explains the problems — unsurmountable, in this case — involved in obtaining a more scientific analysis of the pitch patterns.

Patterns of striking power, tone, and pitch were graphed for the syllables of each of the twenty-eight poems. Contrary to expectation, little distinct correlation between the patterns characterized the three poetic periods of Thomas's poetry. Because the results of the investigation were not significant, graphs of only one poem from each poetic period are reproduced in Appendix II in illustration of the method of analysis attempted. It is suggested, however, that similar studies be undertaken in connection with other poets. A comparative analysis of the patterns of striking power, tone, and pitch in the poetry of contrasted pairs — for example, Thomas and Spender as compared with Auden and Eliot — might well illuminate the auditory techniques of so-called romantic and so-called intellectual poets.

I. AN EXAMINATION OF THE PROBLEM OF PITCH ANALYSIS*

It was one of the original purposes of this study to play all available tapes and records of Dylan Thomas reading his own poems to an instrument which would record graphically the relative variations of the frequencies in his own voice versus time. By analyzing the graphs of audio-frequency, one might throw light upon such problems in Thomas's poetry as the degree of consistency in his readings of a particular poem and the relations between the patterns of audio-frequencies, consonants, vowels, and striking power, as well as the total relation of these four aspects of sound to sense.

Because of the interesting and valuable literary studies which such an instrument of pitch analysis could make possible, it seems appropriate to present here information on this subject.

Conferences with numerous authorities and communication with various laboratories concerned with acoustical problems led to the conclusion that three methods could be used.

So tediously difficult is the first method that a student of literature unfamiliar with the physics of sound could hardly hope to make use of it. It involves the analysis of the oscillographic representation of the spoken word. This process, called Fourier series, represents any wave form in terms of sine and cosine functions — i.e., fundamental and harmonic pitches of the human voice. The approach toward this method is the half-range rule of expansions, which enables one to examine the nonperiodic wave-form[1] by defining any portion of the wave form into a period. This method would also give only sine or cosine terms, depending on choice of reference. The limitation to sine or cosine terms simplifies the solution in that only half the calculations are required. The following is the Fourier series.

* I am particularly indebted to Professor Clifton C. Hill and Mr. James E. Hansen for help in examining the problem of pitch analysis.

[1] The recording of the complete poem would be a nonperiodic function — i.e., the sound patterns would not recur in cycles.

f(t) = the wave form of the spoken word over some finite interval

$$f(t) = \frac{a0}{2} + a_1 \cos 1\omega t + a_2 \cos 2\omega t + a_n \cos n\omega t + \ldots$$
$$b_1 \cos 1\omega t + b_2 \cos 2\omega t + b_n \cos n\omega t + \ldots$$

In this analysis $\frac{a0}{2}$ represents the constant portion of intensity of speech, and, as already mentioned, one set of sine or cosine terms can be eliminated through the proper choice of a suitable axis. The problem encountered is thus the evaluation of the coefficients a_n or b_n, for when these constants are evaluated the analysis is complete. These constants are defined as below:

$$a_n = \frac{1}{\pi} \int_0^P f(t) \cos n\omega t \, d(\omega t)$$

$$b_n + \frac{1}{\pi} \int_0^P f(t) \sin n\omega t \, d(\omega t)$$

0 to *p* (the limits of integration — i.e., the interval of periodicity) define the period chosen. Because of the character of the wave form to be analyzed, the wave form or its derivatives may exhibit sharp discontinuities. It will be necessary, therefore, to carry *n* to high values to obtain convergence of the series. And, too, each value of *n* requires a complete evaluation of the above equation (and will range from 1 to values in the order of thousands). Yet this complex method of half-range expansions is necessary, because the wave form of human speech is a nonperiodic function. It is obvious in the above equations that the function f(t) is not readily defined in an algebraic expression. Therefore the numerical solution will be obligatory. The process will involve integrating small segments of the wave form — i.e., one millisecond per segment — numerically, as explained in *Electrical Engineering Circuits*, Chapter 14.[2] Because of the amount of data (the wave-form — e.g., one side of a record — may be as long as half an hour), this numerical integration process will be most formidable and time-consuming and should be expeditiously evaluated on the IBM type 650 digital computer. If the computer is used, however, it will have to be programmed for the problem — a time-consuming process in itself.

Secondly, a less accurate but perhaps quicker method, the success of which is likely to remain doubtful, is a visual examination of the oscillographic representation of the poem. Since fragments of the output will contain readily definable oscillations, their frequencies might be determined with the aid of accurate time-reference signals simultaneously mposed with the speech on the recording. These time-reference marks

[2] Hugh Hildreth Skilling, *Electrical Engineering Circuits* (New York, John Wiley & Sons, 1961), pp. 403-449.

will enable one to check the time duration between successive crossings, of the time-reference axis, by the wave form. Rather elaborate electronic equipment will be necessary to supply these reference-marks, in addition to highly developed techniques for such a recording. From the data obtained about the crossings, one could then possibly make a relatively accurate conclusion about the fundamental pitch present at that time. This method will enable one only to spot check the wave form where the wave form is most regular. These regularities will occur primarily when simple-toned sounds, such as the vowels, are repeated. Although the method will give only spot checks, it is possible that it might supply a great deal of information. But very expensive oscillographic instruments and many hours of laborious examination of wave forms would be needed.

The third method is to use the Sona-Graph designed by Bell Laboratories and manufactured by Kay Electric Company, Maple Avenue, Pine Brook, New Jersey. This instrument, widely used in measurements of speech, records frequency and intensity versus time. It *may* be ideally suited for the needs of literary studies, but it was not available to the author. Moreover, the Sona-Graph sells for about $ 2,000, and C. G. Conn, Ltd. asserts that its Sona-Graph has proved a "troublesome instrument" and has had to be almost completely rebuilt.[3] The Sona-Graph also requires a considerable amount of maintenance. In view of the expensiveness and questionable performance of the Sona-Graph, it would hardly be advisable to purchase it for any exacting literary study. If, however, one were readily accessible, the instrument might prove useful.

Because the necessary apparatus and skills were not available to the author, it was impossible to carry out any of these three methods. The project involves basically the problem of presenting and recording visual detail that corresponds closely with auditory detail. But with adequate electronic equipment, with a liberal budget, including funds for film for the oscillograph or Sona-Graph, and with the full cooperation of a department of electrical engineering, a future researcher may be successful in analyzing the audio-frequencies of the recorded human voice and in making a valuable contribution to literary studies.

[3] In a letter of March 4, 1959, from Mr. Paul M. Gazlay (Chairman of the Board).

II. GRAPHS OF STRIKING POWER, TONE, AND PITCH

AND DEATH SHALL HAVE NO DOMINION

And death shall have no dominion.
Dead men naked they shall be one
With the man in the wind and the west moon;
When their bones are picked clean and the clean bones gone,
They shall have stars at elbow and foot;
Though they go mad they shall be sane,
Though they sink through the sea they shall rise again;
Though lovers be lost love shall not;
And death shall have no dominion.

And death shall have no dominion.
Under the windings of the sea
They lying long shall not die windily;
Twisting on racks when sinews give way,
Strapped to a wheel, yet they shall not break;
Faith in their hands shall snap in two,
And the unicorn evils run them through;
Split all ends up they shan't crack;
And death shall have no dominion.

And death shall have no dominion.
No more may gulls cry at their ears
Or waves break loud on the seashores;
Where blew a flower may a flower no more
Lift its head to the blows of the rain;
Though they be mad and dead as nails,
Heads of the characters hammer through daisies;
Break in the sun till the sun breaks down,
And death shall have no dominion.

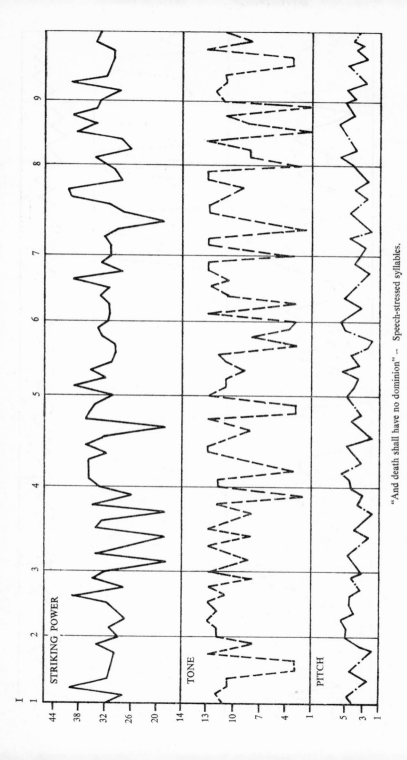

"And death shall have no dominion" – Speech-stressed syllables.

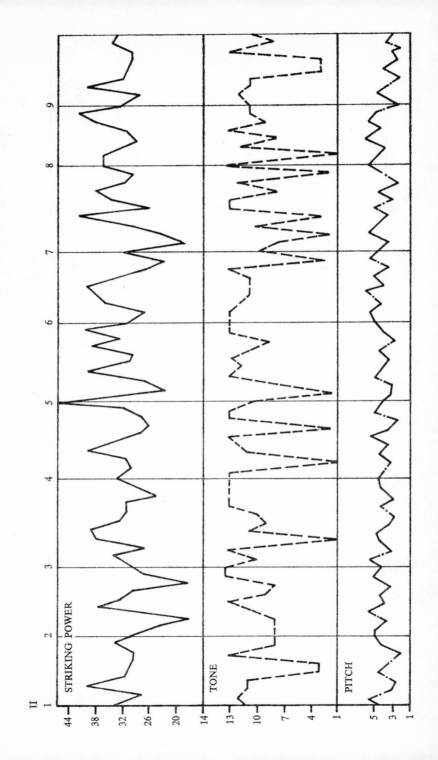

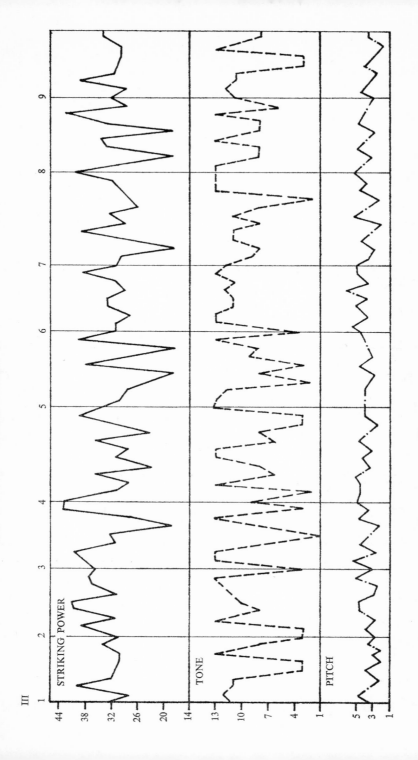

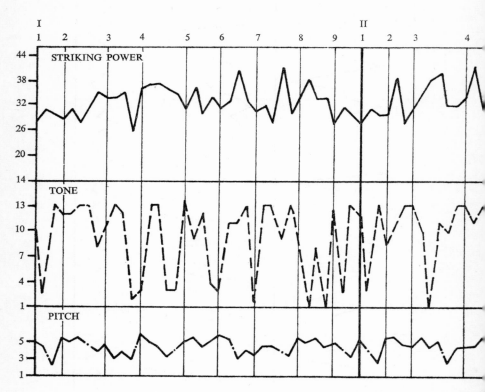

"And death shall have no dominion"

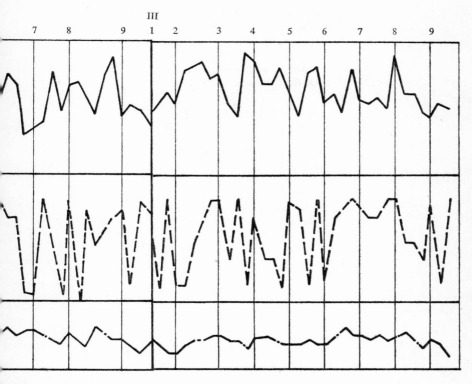

and unstressed syllables.

IN MY CRAFT OR SULLEN ART

In my craft or sullen art
Exercised in the still night
When only the moon rages
And the lovers lie abed
With all their griefs in their arms,
I labour by singing light
Not for ambition or bread
Or the strut and trade of charms
On the ivory stages
But for the common wages
Of their most secret heart.

Not for the proud man apart
From the raging moon I write
On these spindrift pages
Nor for the towering dead
With their nightingales and psalms
But for the lovers, their arms
Round the griefs of the ages,
Who pay no praise or wages
Nor heed my craft or art.

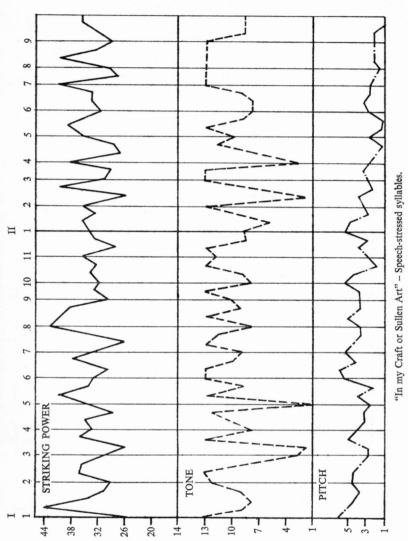

"In my Craft or Sullen Art" – Speech-stressed syllables.

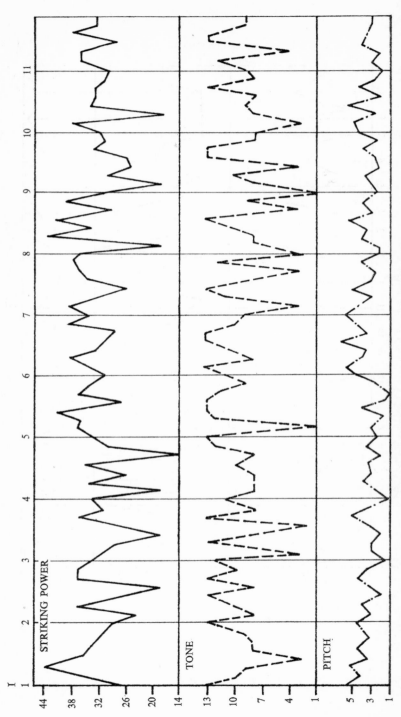

"In my Craft or Sullen Art" — Stressed and unstressed syllables.

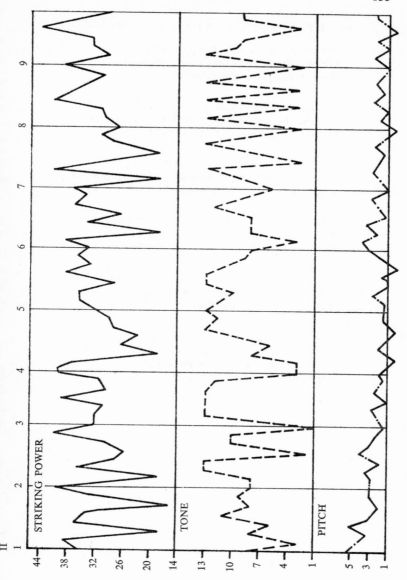

DO NOT GO GENTLE INTO THAT GOOD NIGHT

Do not go gentle into that good night,
Old age should burn and rave at close of day;
Rage, rage against the dying of the light.

Though wise men at their end know dark is right,
Because their words had forked no lightning they
Do not go gentle into that good night.

Good men, the last wave by, crying how bright
Their frail deeds might have danced in a green bay,
Rage, rage against the dying of the light.

Wild men who caught and sang the sun in flight,
And learn, too late, they grieved it on its way,
Do not go gentle into that good night.

Grave men, near death, who see with blinding sight
Blind eyes could blaze like meteors and be gay,
Rage, rage against the dying of the light.

And you, my father, there on the sad height,
Curse, bless, me now with your fierce tears, I pray.
Do not go gentle into that good night.
Rage, rage against the dying of the light.

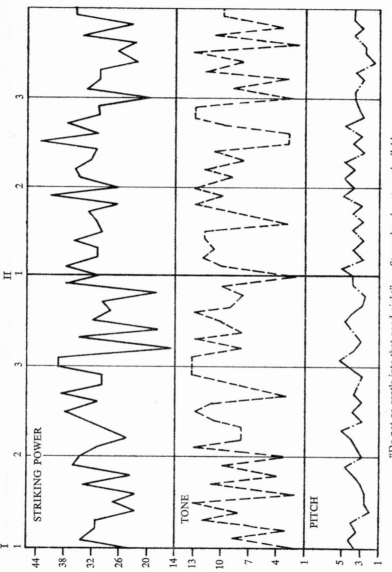

"Do not go gentle into that good night" – Stressed and unstressed syllables.

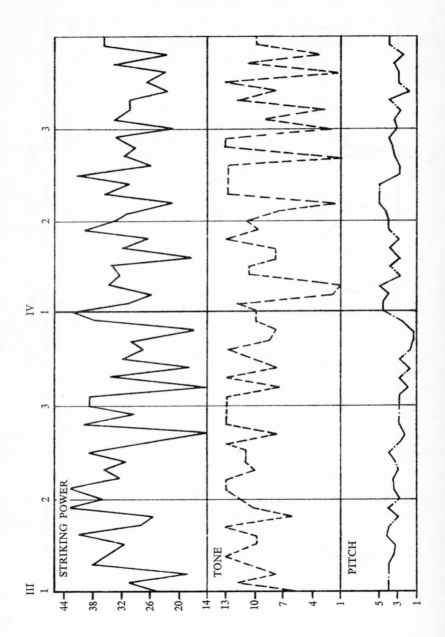

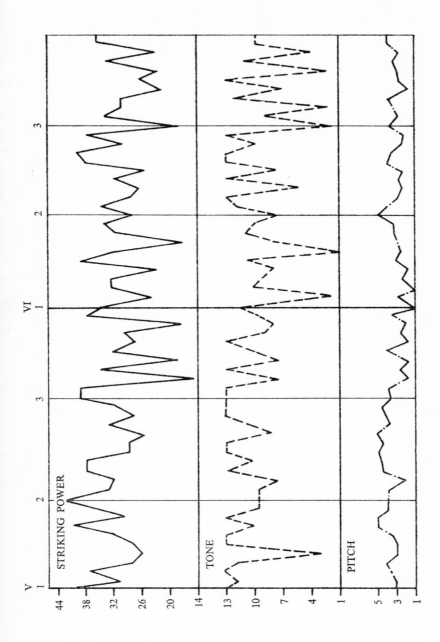

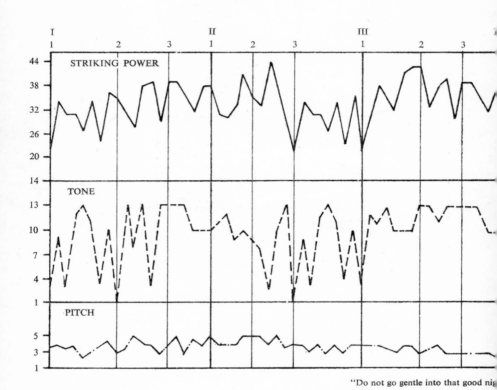

"Do not go gentle into that good nig

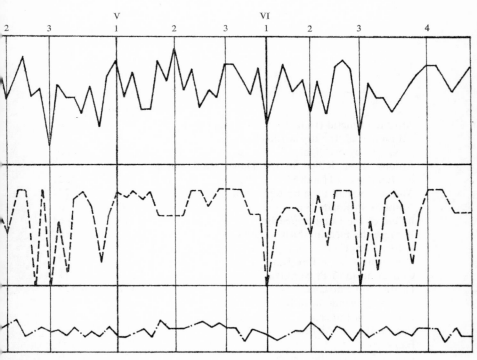

ech-stressed syllables.

III. ALPHABETIZED INDEX OF DYLAN THOMAS'S
COLLECTED POEMS 1934-1952

[1] The form of the titles is that which appears before the respective poems in the Dent edition.

[2] The New Directions edition — although called the Augmented Edition on the paper jacket — adds no new material to the Dent edition and differs only in frontispiece and pagination.

IV. THOMAS'S READING AND RECORDING
ITINERARY IN AMERICA

Most of the following entries are culled from John Malcolm Brinnin's *Dylan Thomas in America.* For one third of them, however, I am even more directly indebted to Professor Brinnin, who was so kind as to compile the requested information for me from his personal, scattered records. Although the listing is probably incomplete, it is the first attempt to reconstruct Thomas's reading and recording itinerary in America.

TRIP I: February 21, 1950 (Tuesday) — May 31, 1950 (Wednesday)

Place	*Date*	*Sponsor*
Kaufmann Auditorium New York, N.Y.	February 23, 1950 (Thursday evening)	The YM-YWHA Poetry Center
Kaufmann Auditorium New York, N.Y.	February 25, 1950 (Saturday evening)	The YM-YWHA Poetry Center
New Haven, Conn.	February 28, 1950 (Tuesday, late afternoon)	Yale University
Cambridge, Mass.[1]	March 1, 1950 (Wednesday afternoon)	Harvard University
Cambridge, Mass.	March 2, 1950 (Thursday morning)	Recordings of his poems for John L. Sweeney's collection in Lamont Library, Harvard University
South Hadley, Mass.	March 2, 1950 (Thursday evening)	Mount Holyoke College
Amherst, Mass.	March 3, 1950 (Friday)	Amherst College

[1] For personal reminiscences of this reading, see Richard Eberhart's "Some Memories of Dylan Thomas", *Yale Literary Magazine*, CXXII (November, 1954), pp. 5-6. This article is reprinted in Tedlock's collection of essays, pp. 55-56.

Place	*Date*	*Sponsor*
Bryn Mawr, Pa.	March 7, 1950 (Tuesday evening)	Bryn Mawr College
The Institute of Contemporary Arts Washington, D.C.	March 8, 1950 (Wednesday evening)	Robert Richman
Washington, D.C.	March 9, 1950 (Thursday morning)	Recordings of his poems at the Library of Congress
New York, N.Y.	March 13, 1950 (Monday)	Columbia University
Ithaca, N.Y.	March 14, 1950 (Tuesday evening)	Cornell University
Gambier, Ohio	March 15, 1950 (Wednesday)	Kenyon College
Chicago, Ill.	March 16, 1950 (Thursday)	The University of Chicago
Notre Dame, Ind.	March 17, 1950 (Friday)	Notre Dame University
Urbana, Ill.	March 20, 1950 (Monday)	The University of Illinois
Iowa City, Iowa	March 21, 1950 (Tuesday)	The State University of Iowa
Berkeley, Cal.	April 4, 1950 (Tuesday)	The University of California
Vancouver, B.C.[2]	April 6, 1950 (Thursday evening)	The University of British Columbia
Seattle, Wash.	April 7, 1950 (Friday)	The University of Washington
Los Angeles, Cal.	April 10, 1950 (Monday)	The University of California at Los Angeles
Claremont, Cal.	April 11, 1950 (Tuesday)	Pomona College
Santa Barbara, Cal.	April 13, 1950 (Thursday)	Santa Barbara Museum and Santa Barbara College
Oakland, Cal.	April 17, 1950 (Monday)	Mills College
San Francisco, Cal.	April 18, 1950 (Tuesday)	San Francisco State College
New York, N.Y.	April 24, 1950 (Monday morning)	Cooper Union
New York, N.Y.	April 24, 1950 (Monday evening)	Museum of Modern Art
Geneva, N.Y.	April 26, 1950 (Wednesday)	Hobart College

[2]   See Floris McLaren's "Dylan Thomas in Vancouver", *Contemporary Verse*, No. 31 (Spring, 1950), pp. 26-27.

Place	Date	Sponsor
Florida Union Auditorium Gainesville,Fla.[3]	April 27, 1950 (Thursday evening, 8:00 p.m.)	The Creative Writing Collection of the University of Florida Library
Wellesley, Mass.	May 1, 1950 (Monday, late afternoon)	Wellesley College
Waltham, Mass.	May 2, 1950 (Tuesday evening)	Brandeis University
Ann Arbor, Mich.	May 3, 1950 (Wednesday)	The University of Michigan
Detroit, Mich.	May 4, 1950 (Thursday)	Wayne State University
Bloomington, Ind.	May 5, 1950 (Friday)	Indiana University
Bloomington, Ind.	May 5, 1950 (Friday)	Indiana University Lecture on his work with British documentary films
Poughkeepsie, N.Y.	May 9, 1950 (Tuesday evening)	Vassar College
Princeton, N.J.	May 10, 1950 (Wednesday)	Princeton University

[3]   From a letter by Gene Baro and from talks with staff members at the University of Florida who attended Thomas's Gainesville reading, the following account is derived: Through the initiative of Gene Baro, the Creative Writing Collection of the University of Florida Library sponsored a lecture by Dylan Thomas. Although Thomas's engagement was originally projected for April 20, 1950, the poet telegraphed Baro from San Francisco to say he was ill and unable to make the scheduled lecture. Since Baro had no address for Thomas, apart from Western Union, he contacted John Malcolm Brinnin and arranged a new date for Thomas's lecture. At 8:00 p.m. on Thursday, April 27, 1950, at the Florida Union Auditorium, Thomas was introduced by Dr. Thomas Pyles and began his readings. Among the selections were poems by Hardy, Yeats, Auden, and Betjeman (including "The Arrest of Oscar Wilde at the Cadogan Hotel"). Of his own works Thomas read only a few, among them, "A Refusal to Mourn the Death, by Fire, of a Child in London". Although publicity was better for Thomas's projected lecture on April 20 than it was for the actual lecture on April 27, the program was rather well attended. No recording was made, because the contract was only for a reading. Thomas stayed in Gainesville at Gene Baro's apartment three or four days. A day or two after the lecture, Baro and Thomas, alone together, read poetry to one another most of the night; the next morning after breakfast Baro persuaded Thomas to make a tape, which is now on deposit in the University Library's Audio-Visual department. The recording is of seven early poems: "From love's first fever to her plague", "Especially when the October wind", "It is the sinners' dust-tongued bell", "'If my head hurt a hair's foot'", "The hand that signed the paper", "Once below a time", and "When all my five and country senses see".

Place	*Date*	*Sponsor*
Kaufmann Auditorium New York, N.Y.	May 15, 1950 (Monday evening)	The YM-YWHA Poetry Center First full recital of prose — selections from *A Portrait of the Artist as a Young Dog*
New York, N.Y.	May 18, 1950 (Thursday)	Barnard College

TRIP II: January 20, 1952 (Sunday) — May 16, 1952 (Friday)

New York, N.Y.	January 30, 1952 (Wednesday)	Columbia University
Kaufmann Auditorium New York, N.Y.	January 31, 1952 (Thursday)	The YM-YWHA Poetry Center
Kaufmann Auditorium New York, N.Y.	February 2, 1952 (Saturday)	The YM-YWHA Poetry Center
New York, N.Y.	February 5, 1952 (Tuesday)	Museum of Modern Art
Washington, D.C.	February 8, 1952 (Saturday)	Institute of Contemporary Arts
New York, N.Y.	February 13, 1952 (Wednesday)	The New School for Social Research
New York, N.Y.	February 14, 1952 (Thursday)	New York University
Burlington, Vt.	February 15, 1952 (Friday)	The University of Vermont
New York, N.Y.	February 18, 1952 (Monday)	Museum of Modern Art
New York, N.Y.	February 21, 1952 (Thursday)	New York University
New York, N.Y.	February 22, 1952 (Friday afternoon)	Recordings of his poems for Caedmon Publishers (TC 1002, Dylan Thomas volume I)
New York, N.Y.	February 24, 1952 (Monday afternoon)	Cherry Lane Theatre
Millbrook, N.Y.	February 26, 1952 (Wednesday)	Bennett Junior College
Montreal, Q.	February 28, 1952 (Friday)	McGill University
New York, N.Y.	February 29, 1952 (Saturday)	Socialist Party
Washington, D.C.	March 1, 1952 (Tuesday)	Institute of Contemporary Arts
Baltimore, Md.	March 4, 1952 (Friday)	The Johns Hopkins University

Place	Date	Sponsor
Princeton, N.J.	March 5, 1952 (Wednesday)	Princeton University
Massachusetts Institute of Technology Auditorium Cambridge, Mass.	March 7, 1952 (Friday)	Massachusetts Institute of Technology Introduction to the reading ("A few Words of a Kind") taped live, poems recorded later in the studio (Caedmon TC 1043, Dylan Thomas volume III)
Lincoln, Mass.	March 7, 1952 (Friday evening)	De Cordova Museum
Brattle Theatre Cambridge, Mass.[4]	March 10, 1952 (Monday evening)	The Poets' Theatre
Boston, Mass.	March 11, 1952 (Tuesday)	Boston University
New York, N.Y.	March 12, 1952 (Wednesday)	The New School for Social Research
Saratoga Springs, N.Y.	March 13, 1952 (Thursday evening)	Skidmore College
New York, N.Y.	March 16, 1952 (Sunday)	Circle-in-the Square Theatre
University Park, Pa.	March 17, 1952 (Monday)	Pennsylvania State University
San Francisco, Cal.	April 3, 1952 (Thursday)	San Francisco State College
Vancouver, B.C.	April 8, 1952 (Tuesday)	University of British Columbia
Vancouver, B.C.	April 9, 1952 (Wednesday)	A local sponsor
Seattle, Wash.	April 10, 1952 (Thursday)	University of Washington
Berkeley, Cal.	April 15, 1952 (Tuesday)	University of California
San Francisco, Cal.	April 16, 1952 (Wednesday)	San Francisco Museum of Art
Salt Lake City, Utah	April 18, 1952 (Friday)	University of Utah
Columbia, Mo.	April 21, 1952 (Monday)	University of Missouri
Chicago, Ill.	April 23, 1952 (Wednesday)	*Poetry Magazine*
Evanston, Ill.	April 24, 1952 (Thursday)	Northwestern University

[4] See Eberhart, pp. 5-6 (in Tedlock, pp. 56-57), for personal reminiscences of this reading.

Place	*Date*	*Sponsor*
Milwaukee, Wis.	April 25, 1952 (Friday)	Marquette University
New Orleans, La.	April 28, 1952 (Monday)	Tulane University

[The only instance of Thomas's failure to fulfill an engagement]

New York, N.Y.	April 30, 1952 (Wednesday)	Masters Institute
(?) Washington, D.C.	(?) May 5, 1952 (Monday)	(?) Institute of Contemporary Arts
Storrs, Conn.	May 7, 1952 (Wednesday evening)	University of Connecticut
Annandale-on-Hudson, N.Y.	May 8, 1952 (Thursday)	Bard College
Bronxville, N.Y.	May 12, 1952 (Monday)	Sarah Lawrence College
Hanover, N.H.	May 13, 1952 (Tuesday)	Dartmouth College
Washington, D.C.	May 14, 1952 (Wednesday)	Duncan Phillips Gallery
Kaufmann Auditorium New York, N.Y.	May 15, 1952 (Thursday evening)	The YM-YWHA Poetry Center Farewell Performance

TRIP III: April 21, 1953 (Tuesday) — June 3, 1953 (Wednesday)

Jordan Hall Boston, Mass.	April 25, 1953 (Saturday evening)	Boston University
Bennington, Vt.	April 27, 1953 (Monday, late afternoon)	Bennington College
Syracuse, N.Y.	April 28, 1953 (Tuesday)	Syracuse University
Williamstown, Mass.	April 29, 1953 (Wednesday)	Williams College
Fogg Museum Harvard University Cambridge, Mass.	May 1, 1953 (Friday)	The Poets' Theatre
Fogg Museum Harvard University Cambridge Mass.	May 3, 1953 (Sunday evening)	The Poets' Theatre The unfinished *Under Milk Wood* presented in a solo performance
Washington, D.C.	May 4, 1953 (Monday)	Institute of Contemporary Arts
Smith Memorial Auditorium Randolph-Macon	May 5, 1953 (Tuesday evening, 8:00 p.m.)	Public Lecture Committee and the Department of English of Randolph-

Place	Date	Sponsor
Woman's College Lynchburg, Va.[5]		Macon Woman's College
Kaufmann Auditorium New York, N.Y.	May 8, 1953 (Friday evening)	The YM-YWHA Poetry Center
Auditorium of the Ethical Culture Society on Rittenhouse Square Philadelphia, Pa.[6]	(?) May 9, 1953 (evening)	Philadelphia Art Alliance
Cambridge, Mass.	May 11, 1953 (Monday evening)	Massachusetts Institute of Technology Introduction to the reading ("A Visit to America") taped live before an audience at MIT, the poems recorded by Station WGBH, Cambridge
Durham, N.C.	May 12, 1953 (Tuesday)	Duke University[7]
Storrs, Conn.	May 13, 1953 (Wednesday evening)	The University of Connecticut
Kaufmann Auditorium New York, N.Y.	May 14, 1953 (Thursday evening)	The YM-YWHA Poetry Center Premiere performance of *Under Milk Wood* (Recorded by Caedmon Publishers on TC 2005)
Amherst, Mass.	May 20, 1953 (Wednesday)	Amherst College

[5] According to Miss W. T. Weathers, no recording of Thomas's lecture was made. But she and a colleague recall that Thomas "did not read a great many of his own poems, and showed a very modest attitude in this respect". After some comments on poetry in general, Thomas read poems by Yeats and possibly by Auden. Of his own poems he read "Fern Hill", "Do not go gentle into that good night", "A Refusal to Mourn the Death, by Fire, of a Child in London", and probably also "The Hunchback in the Park" and "In my Craft or Sullen Art". (From a letter of mid-October, 1961.)

[6] Through the kindness of Daniel G. Hoffman, I am able to summarize from his letter dated November 6, 1961, concerning Thomas's lecture in Philadelphia. He recalls that Thomas prefaced the poems with his prose sketch "A Visit to America" and that among the poems he read were Henry Reed's "Chard Whitlow" and his own "Do not go gentle into that good night" and "Lament". Of Thomas's performance, Professor Hoffman says that "he gave the most electrifying literary program the city has ever known". A recording was made of the lecture, and a copy exists in the archive of Swarthmore College.

[7] See Helen Bevington's *When Found, Make a Verse Of* (New York, Simon and Schuster, 1961), for a personal reminiscence of Thomas at Duke University in 1953.

Place	Date	Sponsor
Kaufmann Auditorium New York, N.Y.	May 24, 1953 (Sunday evening)	The YM-YWHA Poetry Center
Kaufmann Auditorium New York, N.Y.	May 28, 1953 (Thursday)	The YM-YWHA Poetry Center Second performance of *Under Milk Wood*
New York, N.Y.	June 2, 1953 (Tuesday)	Recordings of his poems for Caedmon Publishers (TC 1018, Dylan Thomas volume II)

TRIP IV: October 19, 1953 (Monday) — November 9, 1953 (Monday)

Place	Date	Sponsor
Kaufmann Auditorium New York, N.Y.	October 24, 1953 (Saturday evening)	The YM-YWHA Poetry Center Third performance of *Under Milk Wood*
Kaufmann Auditorium New York, N.Y.	October 25, 1953 (Sunday afternoon)	The YM-YWHA Poetry Center Fourth and greatest performance of *Under Milk Wood* and the last performance of it in which Thomas participated
New York, N.Y.	October 28, 1953 (Wednesday)	City College of New York
New York, N.Y.	October 28, 1953 (Wednesday evening)	Symposium on film art arranged by Cinema 16

BIBLIOGRAPHY

A. PRIMARY SOURCES: WORKS BY DYLAN THOMAS

Adventures in the Skin Trade and Other Stories (Norfolk, Conn., New Directions, 1955).

A Child's Christmas in Wales (Norfolk, Conn., New Directions, 1955).

Collected Poems 1934-1952 (London, J. M. Dent & Sons, Ltd., 1957).

The Collected Poems of Dylan Thomas (New York, New Directions, 1957).

Deaths and Entrances (London, J. M. Dent & Sons, Ltd., 1955).

The Doctor and the Devils (London, J. M. Dent & Sons, Ltd., 1955).

"Dylan Thomas on Reading his Poetry; introduction to a poetry reading", *Mademoiselle*, XLIII (July, 1956), pp. 34-37.

18 Poems (London, The Sunday Referee and The Parton Bookshop, 1934).

In Country Sleep (New York, New Directions, 1952).

Letters to Vernon Watkins. Edited by Vernon Watkins (New York, New Directions, 1957).

The Map of Love: Verse and Prose (London, J. M. Dent & Sons, Ltd., 1939).

New Poems (Norfolk, Conn., New Directions, 1934).

"On Poetry: A Discussion" with James Stephens and Gerald Bullett, *Encounter*, III (November, 1954), pp. 23-26.

"Poetic Manifesto", *Texas Quarterly*, IV (Winter, 1961), pp. 45-53.

Portrait of the Artist as a Young Dog (Norfolk, Conn., New Directions, 1940).

A Prospect of the Sea and other stories and prose writings. Edited by Daniel Jones (London, J. M. Dent & Sons, Ltd., 1957).

Quite Early One Morning (Norfolk, Conn., New Directions, 1954).

Selected Writings of Dylan Thomas. Edited by John L. Sweeney (New York, New Directions, 1946).

"Seven Letters to Oscar Williams (1945-1953)", *New World Writing*, Seventh Mentor Selection (New York, The New American Library of World Literature, Inc., 1955), pp. 128-140.

Twenty-Five Poems (London, J. M. Dent & Sons, Ltd., 1936).

Twenty-Six Poems (London, J. M. Dent & Sons, Ltd., 1950).

Under Milk Wood (Norfolk, Conn., New Directions, 1954).

The World I Breathe (Norfolk, Conn., New Directions, 1939).

B. SECONDARY SOURCES

All secondary sources except *Explicator* items — which are self-explanatory — are briefly annotated.

Some of the following items are reprinted in E. W. Tedlock's *Dylan Thomas: the Legend and the Poet, a Collection of Biographical and Critical Essays* or in J. M. Brinnin's *A Casebook on Dylan Thomas*, or both. One asterisk (*) before an article indicates that it appears in Tedlock, two asterisks (**) that it appears in the *Casebook*, and three asterisks (***) that it appears in both books.

1. Books and Monographs

Arnheim, Rudolf, Auden, W. H., Shapiro, Karl, and Stauffer, Donald A., *Poets at Work: Essays based on the Modern Poetry Collection at the Lockwood Memorial Library, University of Buffalo* (New York, Harcourt, Brace and Company, 1948). [Pp. 53-54, 60, 164, 178-179. Brief notes on Thomas's poetry with a facsimile of a work sheet for the "Ballad of the Long-legged Bait".]

Bayley, John, *The Romantic Survival: A Study of Poetic Evolution* (London, Constable and Company, Ltd., 1957). [Chapter X: "Dylan Thomas", pp. 186-227. A consideration of Thomas's poetic words as "things".]

Bevington, Helen, *When Found, Make a Verse Of* (New York, Simon and Schuster, 1961). [A rich and witty miscellany which includes a personal reminiscence of Dylan Thomas at Duke University in 1953.]

Brinnin, John Malcolm (ed.), *A Casebook on Dylan Thomas* (New York, Thomas Y. Crowell Company, 1960). [A casebook containing ten poems by Thomas, thirty-five reprinted observations and analyses by various authors, and 368 bibliographical entries.]

——, *Dylan Thomas in America: An Intimate Journal* (New York, The Viking Press, 1958). [A record of Thomas's four trips to the United States.]

Bullough, Geoffrey, *The Trend of Modern Poetry* (London, Oliver and Boyd, Inc., 1949). [Pp. 217-221. A criticism and commentary on Thomas's poetry in a chapter entitled "Surrealism, the New Apocalypse".]

Cornell, Kenneth, *The Symbolist Movement* (New Haven, Yale University Press, 1951). [A chronological history of the publications and criticism connected with the Symbolist Movement.]

Day-Lewis, C[ecil], *The Poetic Image* (New York, Oxford University Press, 1947). [Pp. 122-128. A publication of the Clark Lectures given at Cambridge in 1946, containing a discussion of Thomas's imagery, primarily in respect to "After the Funeral".]

Deutsch, Babette, *Poetry in Our Time* (New York, Columbia University Press, 1956). [Pp. viii, pp. 331-347. A commentary on Thomas's poetry.]

Dewey, Godfrey, *Relative Frequency of English Speech Sounds* (Cambridge, Mass., Harvard University Press, 1950). Revised edition. [A study of the relative frequency of vowel and consonant sounds, revealing that a comparatively small part of the commoner words, syllables, or sounds of English form, by their frequent repetitions, a large part of ordinary speech.]

Drew, Elizabeth, and Sweeney, John L., *Directions in Modern Poetry* (New York, W. W. Norton & Company, Inc., 1940). [Pp. 110-112, 184, 201, 221, 252, 258, 263, 279. Brief notes on Thomas's art and craft.]

Durrell, Lawrence, *A Key to Modern British Poetry* (Norman, Okla., The University of Oklahoma Press, 1952). [Chapter X: "Poetry in the Thirties", pp. 196-208. A study in contrasts: Dylan Thomas and William Empson.]

Frankenberg, Lloyd, *Pleasure Dome: On Reading Modern Poetry* (Garden City, N.Y., Doubleday & Company, Inc. [1961]). [A Dolphin Paperback. Part Seven: "Seven Poets", #5 — Dylan Thomas, pp. 325-331. A discussion of Thomas's three approaches to fantasy in his poetry. P. 363. A checklist of principal editions by Thomas. Pp. 374-375. A checklist of principal recordings by Thomas.]

Fraser, G[eorge] S[utherland], *Dylan Thomas* (London, Longmans, Green & Co., Ltd., 1957). [A study of Thomas's poetry which includes frequent references to other criticisms of his poetry.]

Friar, Kimon, and Brinnin, John Malcolm (eds.), *Modern Poetry: American and British* (New York, Appleton-Century-Crofts, Inc., 1951). [Pp. 540-541. A note on Thomas which discusses "Vision and Prayer" and "In Memory of Ann Jones".]

Frye, Northrop (ed.), *Sound and Poetry* (English Institute Essays, 1956. New York, Columbia University Press, 1957). [Six essays on sound and poetry, among them Craig La Drière's "Structure, Sound, and Meaning", pp. 85-108.]

Goodfellow, Dorothy W., "Dylan Thomas, 'The Boy of Summer'", in *Lectures on Some Modern Poets* (=*Carnegie Series in English*, No. 2) (Pittsburg, Carnegie Institute of Technology, 1955), pp. 77-90. [An explication of "I see the boys of summer".]

Graves, Allen Wallace, "Difficult Contemporary Short Stories: William Faulkner, Katherine Anne Porter, Dylan Thomas, Eudora Welty and Virginia Woolf". Unpublished Ph. D. dissertation, University of Washington (1954). [A dissertation which analyzes one "easy" Thomas story — "Patricia, Edith and Arnold" — and two "difficult" ones — "The Burning Baby" and "The Orchards".]

**Graves, Robert, *The Crowning Privilege: Collected Essays on Poetry* (New York, Doubleday & Company, Inc., 1956). [P. 37; from the 1954-1955 Clark Lecture VI, entitled "These Be Your Gods, O Israel!" pp. 119-122, 138-142. A biting criticism of Thomas's poetry as senseless sound.]

***Grigson, Geoffrey, *The Harp of Aeolus and Other Essays on Art, Literature and Nature* (London, George Routledge & Sons, Ltd., 1947). [Chapter XIII: "How Much Me Now Your Acrobatics Amaze", pp. 151-160. A criticism of Thomas's poetry as a "meaningless hot sprawl of mud". Contrast Grigson's more sympathetic treatment of Thomas ten years later in his article, "Recollections of Dylan Thomas", *London Magazine*, IV, September, 1957, pp. 39-45.]

Halperen, Max, "Dylan Thomas: A Soliloquy", *Florida State University Studies*, XI: *Monographs in English and American Literature* (1953), pp. 117-141. [An evaluation of Thomas as a remarkable minor poet limited by repetitious imagery and insufficient range of interest.]

Heppenstall, Rayner, *Four Absentees* (London, Barrie and Rockliff, 1960).

[Personal reminiscences of four dead friends: Dylan Thomas, Eric A. Blair (George Orwell), J. Middleton Murry, and Eric Gill.]

Hoffman, Frederick J., *Freudianism and the Literary Mind* (Baton Rouge, La., Louisiana State University Press, 1945). [Pp. 279, 295-299. Primarily a treatment of three Freudian elements in Thomas's poetry.]

** Holroyd, Stuart, *Emergence from Chaos* (Boston, Houghton Mifflin Company, 1957). [Part II, Chapter I: "Dylan Thomas and the Religion of the Instinctive Life", pp. 77-94. A treatment of Thomas as a primitive whose poetic excellence arose from an engaging simplicity of vision.]

Hornick, Lita, "The Intricate Image: A Study of Dylan Thomas". Unpublished Ph. D. dissertation, Columbia University (1958). [A study of the structure and meaning of Thomas's poems from the standpoint of their imagery.]

Jenkins, David Clay, "Writing in Twentieth Century Wales: A Defense of the Angle-Welsh". Unpublished Ph. D. dissertation, State University of Iowa (1956). A study of Caradoc Evans, Richard Hughes, and Dylan Thomas.]

Jones, Daniel, *An Outline of English Phonetics*, 5th edition (Cambridge, W. Heffer & Sons, Ltd., 1936). [A study of speech sounds: their formation, their attributes, and their relation to other aspects of language.]

——, *The Pronunciation of English*, 4th edition (Cambridge, The University Press, 1956). [A study of the pronunciation of English, with notations of the variations occurring in Scotland and Wales.]

Kaplan, Milton Allen, *Radio and Poetry* (New York, Columbia University Press, 1949). [P. 139. A note referring to Thomas's use of assonance, internal and "slant" rhymes, to enrich the tonal quality of his verse.]

Maud, Ralph Noel, "Language and Meaning in the Poetry of Dylan Thomas", Unpublished Ph. D. dissertation, Harvard University (1958). [A study of language and meaning in Thomas's poetry, with valuable chronologies, bibliographies, and other tables.]

Melchiori, Giorgio, *The Tightrope Walkers: Studies of Mannerism in Modern English Literature* (London, Routledge & Kegan Paul, 1956). [Chapter on "Dylan Thomas: The Poetry of Vision", pp. 213-242; scattered references throughout the book. An examination of Thomas's poetry with special emphasis upon the influences on his style.]

Miles, Josephine, *The Continuity of Poetic Language: Studies in English Poetry from the 1540's to the 1940's* (= *University of California Publications in English*, XIX) (Berkeley and Los Angeles, University of California Press, 1951). [Section III: "The Primary Language of Poetry in the 1940's", pp. 383-542. A listing of Thomas's most used adjectives, nouns, and verbs in the first 1000 lines of his *Selected Writings*; an application of Thomas's count of words to the literary description and evaluation of his poetry.]

Miller, James E., Jr., Shapiro, Karl, and Slote, Bernice. *Start with the Sun: Studies in Cosmic Poetry* (Lincoln, Nebr., The University of Nebraska Press, 1960). [An examination of the Western tradition as seen in the work of Walt Whitman, D. H. Lawrence, Hart Crane, and Dylan Thomas.]

Muir, Edwin, *The Present Age from 1914:* (= *Introductions to Literature*, vol. V) (New York, Robert M. McBride and Company, 1940). [Pp. 128, 220-221. A brief comment on Thomas's poetry.]

Nielsen, Veneta L., *Under Sound: A Theory of Poetry with some Original Poems*

(= *Utah State University Monograph Series*, VII, i) (December, 1958) (Logan, Utah, Utah State University). [A treatment of the subject matter and aesthetic effect of lyric poetry; some original poems.]

Olson, Elder, *The Poetry of Dylan Thomas* (Chicago, The University of Chicago Press, 1954). [A study of Thomas's poetry which includes a controversial astronomical interpretation of the sonnet sequence.]

Osgood, Charles E., *Method and Theory in Experimental Psychology* (New York, Oxford University Press, 1956). Pp. 642-646. A discussion of synesthetic thinking.]

Perrine, Laurence, *Sound and Sense: An Introduction to Poetry* (New York, Harcourt, Brace and Company, 1956). [An approach to the study of poetry. Chapter XIII: "Sound and Meaning", pp. 167-182, contains a catalog of sound-idea correspondences.]

Potter, Ralph Kimball, Kopp, George A., and Green, Harriet C., *Visible Speech* (New York, D. Van Nostrand Company, Inc., 1947). [Chapter II: "The Sound Spectrograph", pp. 8-15, explains the principles and problems involved in various types of sound spectrographs.]

Quennell, Peter, *The Sign of the Fish* (New York, The Viking Press, 1960). [Pp. 41-44. Personal reminiscences of Thomas.]

Read, Herbert, *The True Voice of Feeling: Studies in English Romantic Poetry* (London, Faber and Faber, Ltd., 1953). [P. 86. A comment on Thomas's relation to Hopkins.]

**Rexroth, Kenneth (ed.), *The New British Poets* ([Norfolk, Conn.], New Directions [1949]). [Pp. xvii-xx. A discussion of Thomas's impact upon literature.]

Robson, Ernest M., *The Orchestra of the Language* (New York, Thomas Yoseloff, 1959). [A new approach to non-instrumental phonetics that utilizes instrumental data, the product of twenty years of research into the field of acoustic patterns.]

Rodman, Selden, *100 Modern Poems* (New York, Pellegrini & Cudahy, 1949). [Pp. xxviii-xxx. Notes on Thomas's work.]

Rolph, J. Alexander, *Dylan Thomas: A Bibliography* (New York, New Directions, 1956). [A bibliography of works by Thomas.]

Sanders, Charles, "Poetic Characteristics and Problems of Dylan Thomas" Unpublished M. A. thesis, The University of North Carolina (1958). [A study focusing on the problem of diction in Thomas's poetry.]

Scarfe, Francis, *Auden and After: The Liberation of Poetry 1930-1941* (London, George Routledge and Sons, Ltd., 1943). [Chapter X: "Dylan Thomas: A Pioneer", pp. 101-117. A discussion of Thomas's relationship to Joyce, the Bible, and Freud. Published earlier as "The Poetry of Dylan Thomas", *Horizon*, II, November, 1940, pp. 226-239.]

Schramm, Wilbur Lang, *Approaches to a Science of English Verse* (= *University of Iowa Studies*, No. 46) (Iowa City, Iowa, The University of Iowa, 1935). [An attempt to analyze objectively the melodies and rhythms of verse.]

Scott-James, R. A., *Fifty Years of English Literature, 1900-1950* (London, Longmans, Green and Co., 1958). [Pp. 210-211, 222. Brief references to Thomas and his place among the modern poets.]

Seashore, Carl Emil, *The Psychology of Musical Talent* (Boston, Silver, Burdett and Company, 1919). [Chapter V: "The Sense of Rhythm, pp. 115-126.

A discussion of the nature of rhythm, what rhythm does, and the measurement of the sense of rhythm.]

Sewell, Elizabeth, *The Structure of Poetry* (London, Routledge & Kegan Paul, Ltd., 1951). [Pp. 83, 128. A brief comparison of Thomas's poetry with the poetry of Rimbaud.]

**Sitwell, Edith (ed.), *The Atlantic Book of British and American Poetry* (Boston, Little, Brown and Company, 1958). [Pp. 982-984. A warm appraisal of Thomas's poetry.]

Sonnenschein, E[dward] A[dolf], *What is Rhythm?* (Oxford, Basil Blackwell, 1925). [An attempt to define and analyze rhythm.]

Spender, Stephen, *Poetry Since 1939* (London, Longmans, Green and Co., 1950). [Pp. 44-47. An evaluation of Thomas's poetry.]

Stanford, Derek, *Dylan Thomas: A Literary Study* (London, Neville Spearman, Ltd., 1954). [An examination of Thomas the man and writer.]

Steele, Joshua, *Prosodia Rationalis: An Essay towards establishing the Melody and Measure of Speech, to be expressed and perpetuated by Peculiar Symbols* (London, J. Nichols, 1779). [An attempt to apply the rules of the melody and rhythm of music to the melody and rhythm of language.]

Symons, Arthur, *The Symbolist Movement in Literature* (London, William Heinemann, 1899). [A study of the Symbolist movement in literature with chapters on Rimbaud, Verlaine, Mallarmé.]

Tedlock, E. W. (ed.), *Dylan Thomas: the Legend and the Poet, a Collection of Biographical and Critical Essays* (London, William Heinemann, Ltd., 1960). [A symposium reprinting thirty-eight essays on Thomas.]

Thomas, Caitlin, *Leftover Life to Kill* (New York, Grove Press, Inc. [1959]). [A confession by Thomas's wife of her attempt after his death to escape from her "all-in-Dylan world".]

Tindall, William York, *Forces in Modern British Literature, 1885-1956* Revised edition (New York, Vintage Books, Inc., 1956). [Pp. 236-241. An analysis of Thomas's poetry and a discussion of three main divisions of his career in poetry.]

Treece, Henry, *Dylan Thomas: "Dog Among the Fairies"*. 2nd edition (London, Ernest Benn, Ltd., 1957). [A discussion of the influences on and characteristics of Thomas's poetry.]

Turquet-Milnes, G. [Mrs. Gladys R.], *The Influence of Baudelaire in France and England* (New York, E. P. Dutton and Company, n. d.). [Pp. 251-252. Discussion of "Baudelairian" passages in the works of the Welsh writer Arthur Machen.]

Vogel, Joseph F[rancis], "Religious Thought in the Poetry of Dylan Thomas". Unpublished M. A. thesis, The University of Miami (1960). [A study of the development of Thomas's religious thought as expressed in his poetry.]

Williams, Gwyn, *The Burning Tree: Poems from the First Thousand Years of Welsh Verse* (London, Faber & Faber, 1956). [References in the "Foreward" to Thomas's poetry. The book itself contains forty-seven Welsh poems, or excerpts from Welsh poems, with the modern English translation.]

Yeats, W[illiam] B[utler], *Essays* (New York, The Macmillan Company, 1924). ["Speaking to the Psaltery", pp. 15-32. An essay concerning Yeats' interest in the music of spoken poetry and his experiments with a system of musical notation.]

2. Articles, Reviews, and Memoirs

Adams, Robert Martin, "Taste and bad taste in Metaphysical Poetry: Richard Crashaw and Dylan Thomas", *Hudson Review*, VIII (Spring, 1955), pp. 61-77. [Primarily a consideration of Thomas's sonnets.]

***Adix, Marjorie, "Dylan Thomas: Memories and Appreciations", *Encounter*, II (January, 1954), pp. 13-16. [An account of a conference held by Dylan Thomas with students at the University of Utah in 1952.]

Aiken, Conrad, "The New Euphuism", *New Republic*, CX (January 3, 1944), pp. 26-27. [A review of six new books by New Directions, including Thomas's *New Poems*.]

——, "A Rocking Alphabet", *Poetry*, LVI (June, 1940), pp. 159-161. [A review of *The World I Breathe*.]

*Aivaz, David, "The Poetry of Dylan Thomas", *Hudson Review*, III (Autumn, 1950), pp. 382-404. [A study of Thomas's poetry, with emphasis upon its imagery.]

Arlott, John, "Dylan Thomas", *Spectator*, CXCI (November 13, 1953), p. 534. [An appreciation.]

**Arrowsmith, William, "The Wisdom of Poetry", *Hudson Review*, VI (Winter, 1954), pp. 589-610. [A review of seven volumes of poetry, including Thomas's *Collected Poems*.]

*Barker, George, "Dylan Thomas: Memories and Appreciations", *Encounter*, II (January, 1954), pp. 16-17. [A tribute to Thomas's life; a lament for his early death.]

Baro, Gene, "The Orator of Llareggub", *Poetry*, LXXXVII (November, 1955), pp. 119-122. [A review of *Under Milk Wood*.]

Bartlett, Phyllis, "Thomas' 'Among Those Killed in the Dawn Raid Was a Man Aged One Hundred'", *Explicator*, XII (December, 1953), item 21.

Beardsley, Monroe C., and Hynes, Sam, "Misunderstanding Poetry: Notes on Some Readings of Dylan Thomas", *College English*, XXI (March, 1960), pp. 315-322. [A discussion of four common methods of explication which are of doubtful validity: the anti-explication error; the random method of explication; the bulldozer method of explication; the runic method of explication.]

Berryman, John, "The Loud Hill of Wales", in *The Kenyon Critics: Studies in Modern Literature from the "Kenyon Review"* (Edited by John Crowe Ransom. New York: The World Publishing Company, 1951), pp. 255-259. [A review of *The World I Breathe*.]

Bloom, Edward A., "Dylan Thomas' 'Naked Vision'", *Western Humanities Review*, XIV (Autumn, 1960), pp. 389-400. [A treatment of Thomas's poetic aims as expressed in his poetry and other writings.]

——, and Lillian D., "Dylan Thomas: His Intimations of Mortality", *Boston University Studies in English*, IV (Autumn, 1960), pp. 138-151. [A discussion of Thomas's search for truth and an attempt to integrate Thomas in the intellectual movement associated with the twentieth century.]

Bogan, Louise, "Verse", *New Yorker*, XV (January 27, 1940), pp. 53-54. [A review of *The World I Breathe*, condemning Thomas's poetry as "perfectly hollow".]

——, "Farewell and Hail", *New York Times Book Review* (November 22, 1953), p. 8. [An appreciation.]

Breit, Harvey, "Haunting Drama of Dylan Thomas", *New York Times Magazine* (October 6, 1957), pp. 22-26. [Primarily a consideration of Thomas's public image.]

**——, "Talk with Dylan Thomas", *New York Times Book Review* (May 14, 1950), p. 19. [A talk with Thomas at a Third Avenue bar near the end of his first reading tour in America.]

**——, "Talk with Dylan Thomas", *New York Times Book Review* (February 17, 1952), p. 18. [A talk with Thomas near the beginning of his second reading tour in America. Thomas comments on poetry in general.]

Brooks, Elmer L., "Thomas' 'Among Those Killed in the Dawn Raid Was a Man Aged One Hundred'", *Explicator*, XII (June, 1954), item 49.

Brossard, Chandler, "The Magic of Dylan Thomas", *Commonweal*, LXII (June 10, 1955), pp. 262-263. [A review of *Adventures in the Skin Trade and Other Stories*.]

Brown, Roger W., Black, Abraham H., and Horowitz, Arnold E., "Phonetic Symbolism in Natural Languages", *Journal of Abnormal and Social Psychology*, L (May, 1955), pp. 388-393. [An experiment whose results suggest that some features of phonetic symbolism have a universal validity.]

Cambon, Glauco, "Two Crazy Boats: Dylan Thomas and Rimbaud", *English Miscellany: A Symposium of History, Literature and the Arts*, VII (1956), pp. 251-259. [A discussion of the affinity between Rimbaud's *Bateau Ivre* and Thomas's "Ballad of the Long-legged Bait".]

*Campbell, Roy, "Memories of Dylan Thomas at the B.B.C.", *Poetry*, LXXXVII (November, 1955), pp. 111-114. [Recollections of Thomas the man, the reader, the poet, as Campbell knew him.]

Cane, Melville, "Are Poets Returning to Lyricism?" *Saturday Review*, XXXVII (January 16, 1954), pp. 8-10, 40-41. [A discussion of the intellectual nature of contemporary poetry and a plea for a return to lyricism; a tribute to Christopher Fry and Dylan Thomas as modern romantics.]

Carlson, Helen, "The Overwrought Urn", *Folio*, XXIII (Winter, 1957), pp. 15-24. [A criticism of Thomas's poetry as repetitive and "half-inspired pantheism" which is without true and great dimension.]

Casey, Bill, "Thomas' 'Today, This Insect'", *Explicator*, XVII (March, 1959), item 43.

Chambers, Marlene, "Thomas' 'In the White Giant's Thigh'", *Explicator*, XIX (October, 1960), item 1.

——, "Thomas' 'In the White Giant's Thigh'", *Explicator*, XIX (March, 1961), item 39.

Ciardi, John, "The Real Thomas", *Saturday Review*, XLI (March 1, 1958), pp. 18, 31. [A review of *Letters to Vernon Watkins*.]

——, "Six Hours of Dylan Thomas", *Saturday Review*, XLI (November 15, 1958), p. 50. [A review of Caedmon records of Thomas, Volumes I, II, III, and IV.]

Clair, John A., "Thomas' 'A Refusal to Mourn the Death, by Fire, of a Child in London'", *Explicator*, XVII (December, 1958), item 25.

Condon, Richard A., "Thomas' 'Ballad of the Long-Legged Bait'", *Explicator*, XVI (March, 1958), item 37.

Connolly, Thomas E., "Thomas' 'And Death Shall Have No Dominion'", *Explicator*, XIV (January, 1956), item 33.

Corman, Cid, "Dylan Thomas: Rhetorician in Mid-Career", *Accent*, XIII (Winter, 1953), pp. 56-59. [A review of *Collected Poems*.]

Cox, C. B., "Dylan Thomas's 'Fern Hill'", *Critical Quarterly*, I (Summer, 1959), pp. 134-138. [An appreciative analysis of "Fern Hill".]

Cox, R. G., "The Cult of Dylan Thomas", *Scrutiny*, XVI (September, 1949), pp. 247-250. [A review of *Dylan Thomas* by Henry Treece.]

Cullis, Michael F., "Mr. Thomas and Mr. Auden", *Purpose*, IX (April-June, 1937), pp. 101-104. [A review of *25 Poems*.]

"Current Literature, 1946: Fiction, Drama and Poetry", *English Studies*, XXVIII (June, 1947), pp. 91-92. [A review of *Deaths and Entrances*.]

Daiches, David, "Contemporary Poetry in Britain", *Poetry*, LXII (June, 1943), pp. 150-164. [A consideration of Thomas's influence on the apocalyptic poets.]

——, "The Poetry of Dylan Thomas", *College English*, XVI (October, 1954), pp. 1-8. [A discussion of the development of Thomas's art through three periods of his poetry.]

Davenport, John, "Dylan Thomas", *Twentieth Century*, CLIII (February, 1953), pp. 142-146. [An evaluation of Thomas's poetry.]

——, "Dylan Thomas", *Twentieth Century*, CLIV (December, 1953), pp. 475-477. [An appreciation by a man who knew Thomas for twenty years.]

Davie, Donald, "Correspondence", *The London Magazine*, I (March, 1954), pp. 74-75. [A retort to James Michie who in a letter of tribute to Thomas had claimed to speak for the young generation.]

Davies, Aneirin Talfan, "The Golden Echo", *Dock Leaves*, V (Spring, 1954), pp. 10-17. [Primarily a discussion of the series of four anthologies of modern poems which Thomas compiled and read on the B.B.C. during March, 1953, for the Welsh Home Service.]

Davies, Pennar, "Sober Reflections on Dylan Thomas", *Dock Leaves*, V (Winter, 1954), pp. 13-17. [Adverse criticism of Thomas's poetry as obscure and without moral substance.]

Deutsch, Babette, "Orient Wheat", *Virginia Quarterly Review*, XXVII (Spring, 1951), pp. 221-236. [A commentary on Thomas's poetry. Cf. Deutsch's *Poetry in Our Time*, pp. 331-347.]

Dobrée, Bonamy, "Two Experiments", *Spectator*, CXC (June 12, 1953), pp. 763-764. [A review of *The Doctor and the Devils* and of Jacquetta Hawkes's *Fables*.]

*Durrell, Lawrence, "The Shades of Dylan Thomas", *Encounter*, IX (December, 1957), pp. 56-59. [A lively account of Durrell's memories of Thomas in the late 1930's.]

*Eberhart, Richard, "Some Memories of Dylan Thomas", *Yale Literary Magazine*, CXXII (November, 1954), pp. 5-6. [Personal reminiscences of Thomas at Cambridge, Massachusetts, in early March, 1950, and in mid-March, 1952.]

"Editorial Note: The Second Phase of Neo-Romanticism", *Poetry and Poverty*, IV (1953), pp. 2-7. [A short discussion of Thomas's poetic virtues and vices.]

Edman, Irwin, "The Spoken Word", *Saturday Review*, XXXV (November 29, 1952), pp. 68-69. [A review of Caedmon record of Thomas, volume I.]

**Empson, William, "Books in General", *New Statesman and Nation*, XLVII (May 15, 1954), pp. 635-636. [A review of *Collected Poems* and *Under Milk Wood*.]

——, "To Understand a Modern Poem", *Strand*, CXII (March, 1947), pp. 60-64. [An explication of "A Refusal to Mourn the Death, by Fire, of a Child in London".]

Essig, Erhardt H., "Thomas' 'Sonnet I' ('Altarwise by Owl-Light')", *Explicator*, XVI (June, 1958), item 53.

Evans, Oliver, "Dylan Thomas' Birthday Poems". Type-written MS. [An analysis and evaluation of "Twenty-four years", "Poem in October", and "Poem on his Birthday".]

——, "The Making of a Poem: Dylan Thomas' 'Do not go gentle into that good night'", *English Miscellany: A Symposium of History, Literature and the Arts*, VI (1955), pp. 163-173. [A discussion — based on the work sheets, which are partially reproduced in eight plates — of Thomas's method of composing this villanelle.]

——, "The Making of a Poem (II): Dylan Thomas' 'Lament'", *English Miscellany: A Symposium of History, Literature and the Arts*, VII (1956), pp. 241-249. [An analysis of "Lament".]

F[itts], D[udley], "The New Books", *Saturday Review of Literature*, XXII (May 11, 1940), p. 20. [A review of several new books, including Thomas's *The World I Breathe*.]

Fox, Charles Warren, "An Experimental Study of Naming", *American Journal of Psychology*, XLVII (October, 1935), pp. 545-579. [An experiment demonstrating that persons tend to associate such sounds as *i*, *z*, and *k* with sharpness or angularity and such sounds as *m*, *l*, *u*, and *b* with smoothness or voluminousness.]

Frankenberg, Lloyd, "Controlled Abandon", *New York Times Book Review* (April 6, 1952), p. 4. (A review of *In Country Sleep*.]

*Fraser, G. S., "The Artist as a Young Dog", *New Statesman and Nation*, XLIX (June 11, 1955), p. 812. [Personal reminiscences of Thomas and a commentary on Emlyn Williams's performance at the Globe Theatre of "A Boy Growing Up", a portrayal of the characters in Thomas's prose works.]

——, "Craft and Sullen Art", *New Statesman and Nation*, XLIV (November 29, 1952), pp. 640, 642. [A review of *Collected Poems*.]

Gant, Roland, "Romantics and Others", *Poetry Review*, XXXIV (May-June, 1943), pp. 179-182. [Two brief references to Thomas in this discussion of Celtic poets.]

Gardiner, Harold C., "Welsh Chanter's Spell", *America*, XCII (January 1, 1955), p. 363. [A review of *Quite Early One Morning*.]

Garlick, Raymond, "The Endless Breviary: Aspects of the Work of Dylan Thomas", *The Month* (London), II (March, 1954), pp. 143-153. [An examination of Thomas's poetry in respect to Welsh and Christian traditions.]

Garrigue, Jean, "Dark is a Way and Light is a Place", *Poetry*, XCIV (May, 1959), pp. 111-114. [A review of *Collected Poems*.]

Ghiselin, Brewster, "Critical Work in Progress", *Poetry*, LXXXVII (November,

1955), pp. 118-119. [A review of *The Poetry of Dylan Thomas* by Elder Olson.]

——, "Use of a Mango", *Rocky Mountain Review* [now *Western Review*], VIII (Spring, 1944), pp. 111-112. [A review of *New Poems*.]

*Gibson, Henry, " A Comment", *The Critic*, I (Autumn, 1947), pp. 19-20. [A commentary on "A Refusal to Mourn the Death, by Fire, of a Child in London" and "We lying by seasand".]

Giovannini, G., "Thomas' 'The force that through the green fuse' ", *Explicator*, VIII (June, 1950), item 59.

*Graddon, John, "The Interior Life", *Poetry Review*, XLIV (April-June, 1953), pp. 338-340. [A favorable review of *Collected Poems* paired with Geoffrey Johnson's unfavorable review of the volume.]

**Gregory, Horace, "Romantic Heritage in the Writings of Dylan Thomas", *Yale Literary Magazine*, CXXII (November, 1954), pp. 30-34. [An essay on "neo-romanticism" and Thomas, reprinted, with changes, from *Poetry* LXIX, March, 1947, pp. 326-336.]

Grenander, M. E., "Sonnet V from Dylan Thomas' 'Altarwise by Owl-Light Sequence' ", *Notes and Queries*, New Series V (June, 1958), p. 263. [A consideration of the Ishmael image in Sonnet V.]

**Grigson, Geoffrey, "Recollections of Dylan Thomas", *London Magazine*, IV (September, 1957), pp. 39-45. [Recollections of Thomas with friends Norman Cameron, Bernard Spencer, Geoffrey Grigson, Ruthven Todd.]

Hamilton, Edith, "Words, Words, Words; The Modern School of Verse", *Saturday Review*, XXXVIII (November 19, 1955), pp. 15-16, 52-53. [A scathing criticism of Thomas's poetry as dark, ugly, meaningless.]

Harding, Joan, "Dylan Thomas and Edward Thomas", *Contemporary Review*, CXCII (September, 1957), pp. 150-154. [A comparison and contrast of Dylan Thomas and Edward Thomas.]

**Hardwick, Elizabeth, "America and Dylan Thomas", *Partisan Review*, XXIII (Spring, 1956), pp. 258-264. [A commentary on Dylan Thomas and America generally and on John Malcolm Brinnin's *Dylan Thomas in America* specifically.]

Hassan, Ihab H., "Thomas' 'The Tombstone Told When She Died' ", *Explicator*, XV (November, 1956), item 11.

Hawkes, Terence, "Dylan Thomas's Welsh", *College English*, XXI (March, 1960), pp. 345-347. [A discussion of Thomas's use of Welsh idioms, especially those with bawdy connotations which contribute to the humor in *Under Milk Wood*.]

Hecht, Roger, "Light and Darkness", *Bard Review*, II (Spring, 1947), pp. 57-58. [A review of *The Selected Writings of Dylan Thomas*, edited by John L. Sweeney.]

Heseltine, Nigel, "Dylan Thomas", *Wales*, II (August, 1937), pp. 74-75. [A review of *25 Poems*.]

Hewes, Henry, "And Death shall have no dominion", *Saturday Review*, XL (October 19, 1957), p. 53. [A review of Emlyn Williams's performance at the Globe Theatre of "A Boy Growing Up", a portrayal of the characters in Thomas's prose works.]

Highet, Gilbert, "The Great Welsh Poet: Dylan Thomas. An Excerpt from *The Powers of Poetry*", *Vogue*, CXXXV (March 15, 1960), pp. 110-111,

152-154. [An examination of the peculiar characteristics of the Welsh
people and their relationship to Thomas himself and to his poetry.]

*Horan, Robert, "In Defense of Dylan Thomas", *Kenyon Review*, VII (Spring,
1945), pp. 304-310. [An evaluation of Thomas's poetry.]

Howard, D. R., "Then I Slept", *Renascence*, IX (Winter, 1956), pp. 91-96.
[A review of *A Child's Christmas in Wales*, John Malcolm Brinnin's *Dylan
Thomas in America*, and *Poetry*, LXXXVII, November, 1955, A Dylan
Thomas Number.]

——, "Thomas' 'In My Craft or Sullen Art'", *Explicator*, XII (February,
1954), item 22.

Huddlestone, Linden, "An Approach to Dylan Thomas", in *New Writing*
(Edited by John Lehmann. London, Penquin Books, Ltd., 1948), pp.
123-160. [An appraisal of Thomas's poetry, with emphasis upon his "style
of sound".]

Hynes, Sam, "Thomas' 'From Love's First Fever to her Plague'", *Explicator*,
IX (December, 1950), item 18.

"In the White Giant's Thigh", from "Letters to and from the Editor", *Atlantic*,
CLXXXVIII (November, 1951), pp. 22-23. [Five letters and the editors'
note concerning the publication in the September issue of *Atlantic* of "In
the White Giant's Thigh".]

John, Augustus, "Dylan Thomas and Company", *Sunday Times* (London),
September 28, 1958, p. 17. [Personal reminiscences of Thomas. A revised
and condensed version of this article appears in *A Casebook on Dylan
Thomas*, pp. 276-278.]

*Johnson, Geoffrey, "The Acid Test", *Poetry Review*, XLIV (April-June, 1953),
pp. 340-343. [An unfavorable review of *Collected Poems* paired with John
Graddon's favorable review of the volume.]

***Johnson, Pamela Hansford, "A Memoir", *Adam International Review*,
No. 238 (1953), pp. 24-25. [Recollections of the youthful Thomas.]

Johnson, S. F., "Thomas' 'The force that through the green fuse'", *Explicator*,
VIII (June, 1950), item 60.

——, "Thomas' 'The force that through the green fuse'", *Explicator*, X
(February, 1952), item 26.

——, "Thomas' 'The Hunchback in the Park' and 'The Marriage of a Virgin'",
Explicator, X (February, 1952), item 27.

***Jones, Daniel, "Dylan Thomas: Memories and Appreciations", *Encounter*,
II (January, 1954), pp. 9-10. [An account of Jones's childhood intimacy
with Thomas and some comments on autobiographical incidents in
Thomas's prose.]

Jones, Glyn, "Dylan Thomas", *Welsh Review*, II (October, 1939), pp. 179-180.
[A review of *The Map of Love*.]

——, "Dylan Thomas and Welsh", *Dock Leaves*, V (Spring, 1954), pp. 24-25.
[A consideration of the Welsh characteristics in Thomas's poetry as the
result either of accident or of the influence upon him of Hopkins.]

Jones, Noel A., "Dylan Thomas as a Pattern", in *British Annual of Literature*,
VI (London, The British Author's Press, 1949), pp. 12-16. [A presentation
of the problems involved in evaluating Thomas's writings.]

Jones, Robert C., "Thomas' 'The Conversation of Prayer'", *Explicator*, XVII
(April, 1959), item 49.

Julian, Sister Mary, "Edith Sitwell and Dylan Thomas: Neo-Romantics", *Renascence*, IX (Spring, 1957), pp. 120-126, 131. [An evaluation of Thomas's poetry and prose.]

Karwoski, T. F., Odbert, H. S., and Osgood, C. E., "Studies in Synesthetic Thinking: II. The Role of Form in Visual Responses to Music", *Journal of General Psychology*, XXVI (1942), pp. 199-222. [An analysis of the relation between the mood of music and the colors suggested by that music.]

Knauber, Charles F., "Imagery of Light in Dylan Thomas", *Renascence*, VI (Spring, 1954), pp. 95-96, 116. [An examination of Thomas's poetry as his "individual struggle from darkness towards some measure of light".]

Knieger, Bernard, "Thomas' 'Light Breaks where no Sun Shines'", *Explicator* XV (February, 1957), item 32.

——, "Thomas' 'Love in the Asylum'", *Explicator*, XX (October, 1961), item 13.

——, "Thomas' 'On the Marriage of a Virgin'", *Explicator*, XIX (May, 1961), item 61.

——, "Thomas' 'Sonnet I'", *Explicator*, XV (December, 1956), item 18.

——, "Thomas' 'Sonnet II'", *Explicator*, XVIII (November, 1959), item 14.

——, "Thomas' 'Sonnet III'", *Explicator*, XVIII (January, 1960), item 25.

——, "Thomas' 'Twenty-four Years'", *Explicator*, XX (September, 1961), item 4.

Korg, Jacob, "Imagery and Universe in Dylan Thomas's '18 Poems'", *Accent*, XVII (Winter, 1957), pp. 3-15. [A consideration of the imagery in *18 Poems* in respect to Thomas's view of the universe as complex and paradoxical.]

Lander, Clara, "With Welsh and Reverent Rook: the Biblical Element in Dylan Thomas", *Queen's Quarterly*, LXV (Autumn, 1958), pp. 437-447. [A discussion of Thomas's relation to and use of the Bible.]

Laurentia, Sister M., "Thomas' 'Fern Hill'", *Explicator*, XIV (October, 1955), item 1.

*Lewis, E. Glyn, "Dylan Thomas", *Welsh Review*, VII (Winter, 1948), pp. 270-281. [A treatment of Thomas as an essentially religious poet.]

——, "Some Aspects of Anglo-Welsh Literature", *Welsh Review*, V (Autumn, 1946), pp. 176-186. [A discussion of the three important periods of Anglo-Welsh literature and the contribution of Anglo-Welsh literature to the main body of English literature; an examination of the relationship between seventeenth century and contemporary Anglo-Welsh poetry, with special reference to Dylan Thomas.]

Lewis, Saunders, "Dylan Thomas", *Dock Leaves*, V (Spring, 1954), pp. 8-9. [A talk broadcast in Welsh over the B.B.C. the day after Thomas's death. Page 9 is a translation of the talk.]

Lougée, David, "An Open Window", *Poetry*, XCIV (May, 1959), pp. 114-117. [A review of *Letters to Vernon Watkins*.]

——, "The Worlds of Dylan Thomas", *Poetry*, LXXXVII (November, 1955), pp. 114-115. [A review of *Quite Early One Morning* and *Adventures in the Skin Trade and Other Stories*.]

M., G., "Worth Reprinting", *New Republic*, CXV (December 2, 1946), p. 742. [A review of *The Selected Writings of Dylan Thomas*, edited by John L. Sweeney.]

Macgregor-Hastie, Roy, "Ricordo di Dylan Thomas", *Ausonia*, XIV, i (January-February, 1959), pp. 61-64. [A memory of Dylan Thomas, published in Italian.]

***MacNeice, Louis, "Dylan Thomas: Memories and Appreciations", *Encounter*, II (January, 1954), pp. 12-13. [A tribute.]

——, "Sometimes the Poet Spoke in Prose", *New York Times Book Review* (December 19, 1954), p. 1. [A review of *Quite Early One Morning*.]

——, "The Strange, Mighty Impact of Dylan Thomas' Poetry", *New York Times Book Review* (April 5, 1953), pp. 1, 17. [A review of *Collected Poems*.]

Mankowitz, Wolf, "Dylan Thomas", *Scrutiny*, XIV (Summer, 1946), pp. 62-67. [A review of *Deaths and Entrances*.]

Mathias, Roland, "A Merry Manshape (or Dylan Thomas at a distance)", *Dock Leaves*, V (Spring, 1954), pp. 30-39. [An appraisal of Thomas's poetry.]

Maud, Ralph N[oel], "Dylan Thomas' *Collected Poems:* Chronology of Composition", *PMLA*, LXXVI (June, 1961), pp. 292-297. [A chronology, based mainly on extant Thomas notebooks for the years 1930 to 1934, that reveals the delayed publication of many early poems.]

——, "Dylan Thomas' First Published Poem", *Modern Language Notes*, LXXIV (February, 1959), pp. 117-118. [A bibliographical note that an early form of "And death shall have no dominion", published in *The New English Weekly, May* 18, 1933, is Thomas's first publication outside Swansea.]

——, "Dylan Thomas Manuscripts in Houghton Library", *Audience*, I (February 4, 1955), pp. 4-6. [An article on the two most important MSS. which Oscar Williams presented to Harvard University: 166 written sides of work sheets for Prologue; 65 written sides for "Over Sir John's Hill".]

——, "Dylan Thomas's Poetry", in *Essays in Criticism*, IV (Oxford, Basil Blackwell, 1954), pp. 411-420. [An analysis of the craftsmanship of Thomas's poems.]

——, "A Note on Dylan Thomas's Serious Puns", *Audience*, VI (April 15, 1955), pp. 5-7. [An examination of some serious puns in Thomas's poetry which are pertinent to his basic themes.]

——, "Obsolete and Dialect Words as Serious Puns in Dylan Thomas", *English Studies*, XLI (February, 1960), pp. 28-30. [Essentially the same as Maud's article in *Audience*, "A Note on Dylan Thomas's Serious Puns", *q.v.*]

——, "Thomas' 'Sonnet I'", *Explicator*, XIV (December, 1955), item 16.

McLaren, Floris, "Dylan Thomas in Vancouver", *Contemporary Verse*, No. 31 (Spring, 1950), pp. 26-27. [An account of Thomas's speaking engagements in Vancouver on April 6, 1950.]

McLuhan, Herbert Marshall, "Sight, Sound, and the Fury", *Commonweal*, LX (April 9, 1954), pp. 7-11. [A reference to the influence on Thomas's later poetry of his reading poetry on the radio.]

——, "Space, Time and Poetry", *Explorations*, IV (February, 1955), pp. 56-62. [A reference to Thomas's poetry as illustration of the theory that poetry which develops the visual image intensely also tends strongly towards the auditory stress.]

***Merwin, W[illiam] S., "The Religious Poet", *Adam International Review*,

No. 238 (1953), pp. 73-78. [A discussion of Thomas as an essentially religious poet.]

Meyerhoff, Hans, "The Violence of Dylan Thomas", *New Republic*, CXXXIII (July 11, 1955), pp. 17-19. [A review of *Adventures in the Skin Trade and other stories*.]

Michie, James, "Correspondence", *The London Magazine*, I (February, 1954), pp. 77-99. [An attempt to explain what Thomas and his poetry meant to Michie's young generation.]

Miller, George A., "Speech and Language", in *Handbook of Experimental Psychology* (Edited by S. S. Stevens. New York, John Wiley & Sons, Inc., 1951), pp. 789-810. [A study showing that the greater frequency of occurrence of certain speech sounds results from their being easier to produce and easier to discriminate than certain other sounds.]

Miller, James E., Jr., "Four Cosmic Poets", *University of Kansas City Review*, XXIII (June, 1957), pp. 312-320. [A discussion of four cosmic poets: Walt Whitman, D. H. Lawrence, Hart Crane, and Dylan Thomas.]

Mizener, Arthur, "Poets", *Nation*, CLXIII (August 10, 1946), p. 160. [A review of Henry Treece's *Collected Poems* with some comments on Thomas's influence on Treece.]

"Modernism in Poetry Yes and No — Readers' Free-for-All", *Poetry Review*, XLIV (October-December, 1953), pp. 454-456. [Five readers express their reactions to John Graddon's and Geoffrey Johnson's contrasting reviews of Thomas's *Collected Poems*.]

Montague, Gene, "Thomas' 'To-day, This Insect'", *Explicator*, XIX (December, 1960), item 15.

*Moore, Geoffrey, "Dylan Thomas: Significance of His Genius", *Kenyon Review*, XVII (Spring, 1955), pp. 258-277. [An evaluation of Thomas's poetry.]

Moore, Nicholas, "The Poetry of Dylan Thomas", *Poetry Quarterly*, X (Winter, 1948), pp. 229-236. [A consideration of Thomas's poetic virtues and vices in respect to his craftsmanship and his themes.]

Morgan, W. John, "Evans, Thomas and Lewis", *Twentieth Century*, CLX (October, 1956), pp. 322-329. [A discussion of the need for preserving or reviving rural, Northern Welsh culture, with special mention of *Under Milk Wood*.]

Moynihan, William T., "The Auditory Correlative", *Journal of Aesthetics and Art Criticism*, XVII (September, 1958), pp. 93-102. [A thoughtful analysis of the "auditory correlative" of the literal meaning in poetry, with examples from several poems by Thomas.]

——, "Dylan Thomas' 'Hewn Voice'", *Texas Studies in Literature and Language*, I (Autumn, 1959), pp. 313-326. [An examination of three types of auditory techniques which Thomas employed to enable the sound to support or echo the sense in his poetry.]

——, "Thomas' 'In the White Giant's Thigh'", *Explicator*, XVII (May, 1959), item 59.

——, "Thomas' 'Light Breaks Where No Sun Shines'", *Explicator*, XVI (February, 1958), item 28.

"Mr. Dylan Thomas: Innovation and Tradition", *Times* (London), November 10, 1953, p. 11. [An obituary — probably the best one written.]

Muecke, D. C., "Come Back! Come Back! — A Theme in Dylan Thomas's Prose", *Meanjin*, XVIII (April, 1959), pp. 69-76. [A discussion of the theme in Thomas's prose of losing someone or being unable to recapture something.]

Muir, Edwin, "The Art of Dylan Thomas", *Harper's Bazaar*, LXXXVIII (February, 1954), p. 128. [A memorial tribute.]

——, "New Poetry", *Purpose*, XI (October-December, 1939), pp. 241-243. [A review of *The Map of Love*.]

"Obituary", *New York Times*, November 10, 1953, p. 31. [An obituary containing a general criticism of Thomas's work.]

Ochshorn, Myron, "The Love Song of Dylan Thomas", *New Mexico Quarterly*, XXIV (Spring, 1954), pp. 46-65. [A treatment of Thomas's poetry as a record of the struggle toward a life in which love can exist.]

Odbert, H. S., Karwoski, T. F., and Eckerson, A. B., "Studies in Synesthetic Thinking: I. Musical and Verbal Association of Color and Mood", *Journal of General Psychology*, XXVI (1942), pp. 153-173. [An experiment to investigate the form factor in color-hearing.]

Olson, Elder, "The Poetry of Dylan Thomas", *Poetry*, LXXXIII (January, 1954), pp. 213-220. [A review of *Collected Poems*.]

"Passionate Pilgrim", *Time*, XLVIII (December 2, 1946), pp. 112, 114, 116. [A review of *The Selected Writings of Dylan Thomas*, edited by John L. Sweeney.]

Peel, J. H. B., "The Echoes in the Booming Voice", *New York Times Book Review* (October 20, 1957), pp. 40-41. [A study of Hopkins and Thomas, treating Hopkins as an inventor and major poet and Thomas as an imitator and minor poet.]

"Poetry and Protest", *Poetry and Poverty*, IV (1953), pp. 39-40. [A review of *Collected Poems*.]

Prys-Jones, A. G., "Death Shall Have No Dominion", *Dock Leaves*, V (Spring, 1954), pp. 26-29. [A tribute paid to Thomas at the Memorial Recital organized by the Cardiff Branch of the Poetry Association, at the Reardon Smith Lecture Theatre, December 7, 1953.]

Raine, Kathleen, "Dylan Thomas", *New Statesman and Nation*, XLVI (November 14, 1953), p. 594. [A tribute and memory of Thomas, with emphasis on his early poetic career.]

***Reid, Alastair, "A First Word", *Yale Literary Magazine*, CXXII (November, 1954), p. 20. [Personal reminiscences of Thomas's delight in words.]

Rhys, Aneurin, "Letters to the Editor: Dylan Thomas — A Further Estimate", *Poetry Review*, XXXIX (April-May, 1948), pp. 214-216. [An adversely critical essay which attacks Thomas's poetry on the grounds of "verbal trickery" and obscurity.]

Rhys, Keidrych, "Contemporary Welsh Literature", in *The British Annual of Literature, 1946* (London, The British Authors' Press, Ltd. [1946]), pp. 17-22. [A discussion of the "Welsh Renaissance", with several references to Thomas.]

Rickey, Mary Ellen, "Thomas' 'The Conversation of Prayer'", *Explicator*, XVI (December, 1957), item 15.

Riggs, Thomas, Jr., "Recent Poetry — a Miscellany", *Nation*, CLXXVI (May 2, 1953), pp. 376-378. [A review of *Collected Poems*.]

*Roethke, Theodore, "Dylan Thomas: Memories and Appreciations", *Encounter*, II (January, 1954), p. 11. [An account of Thomas as Roethke knew him — from 1950 on — with special mention of Thomas's literary knowledge and preferences.]

Rolo, Charles J., "Reader's Choice", *Atlantic Monthly*, CXCII (November, 1953), pp. 110-111. [A review of *The Doctor and the Devils*.]

Rosenfeld, Paul, "Decadence and Dylan Thomas", *Nation*, CL (March 23, 1940), pp. 399-400. [A review of *The World I Breathe*.]

*Rothberg, Winterset [Theodore Roethke], "One Ring-tailed Roarer to Another", *Poetry*, LXXXI (December, 1952), pp. 184-186. [A review of *In Country Sleep and other poems*, written at Thomas's request.]

*Rousillat, Suzanne, "His Work and Background", *Adam International Review*, No. 238 (1953), pp. 66-72. [The fullest detailed account of Thomas's life.]

"Salute to a Poet", *Times* (London) *Literary Supplement*, November 28, 1952, p. 776. [A review of *Collected Poems;* a favorable and detailed examination of Thomas's poetry.]

Sapir, Edward, "A Study in Phonetic Symbolism", *Journal of Experimental Psychology*, XII (June, 1929), pp. 225-239. [A study, of the symbolic suggestiveness of special sound contrasts, which revealed that certain vowels and certain consonants "sound bigger" than others.]

*Savage, D. S., "The Poetry of Dylan Thomas", *New Republic*, CXIV (April 29, 1946), pp. 618, 620, 622. [A survey of Thomas's poetic development through the publication of *Deaths and Entrances*.]

***Scarfe, Francis, "The Poetry of Dylan Thomas", *Horizon*, II (November, 1940), pp. 226-239. [A discussion of Thomas's relationship to Joyce, the Bible, and Freud. Identical to Chapter X in Scarfe's *Auden and After, q.v.*]

**Scott, Winfield Townley, "Death, and Some Dominions of It", *Yale Literary Review*, CXXII (November, 1954), pp. 13-14. [An essay on the effect of death on a poet's public image, in particular on Thomas's.]

——, "The Lyric Marvel", *Saturday Review*, XXXVIII (January 8, 1955), pp. 17-18. [A review of *Quite Early One Morning*.]

——, "Wild Man Bound", *Saturday Review*, XXXVI (April 11, 1953), pp. 29-30. [A review of *Collected Poems*.]

Seldes, Gilbert, "Radio, TV, and the Common Man", in *Is the Common Man Too Common? An Informal Survey of Our Cultural Resources and What We are Doing about Them.* (Edited by Joseph Wood Krutch *et al.* Norman, Okla., The University of Oklahoma Press, 1954), pp. 45-55. [An inquiry, by an authority on mass media, into the relation between the broadcasters and the public.]

Seymour, William Kean [unsigned]. "Poets and Pretenders", *Poetry Review*, XXXVII (April-May, 1946), pp. 128-129. [A review of *Deaths and Entrances*.]

***Shapiro, Karl, "Dylan Thomas", *Poetry*, LXXXVII (November, 1955), pp. 100-110. [A critical treatment of Thomas's poetry, with a list of the thirty poems which Shapiro feels belong to the permanent body of any poetry.]

**Shuttleworth, Martin, "Without Apologies", *New Statesman and Nation*, XLV (February 7, 1953), pp. 144-145. [A stinging observation of a par-

ticular "literary" luncheon held in honor of Thomas's receipt of the Foyle
Award.]

*Sitwell, Edith, "Comment on Dylan Thomas", *The Critic*, I (Autumn, 1947),
pp. 17-18. [An appreciation of Thomas's poetry, including a favorable
commentary on "We lying by seasand" and "A Refusal to Mourn the
Death, by Fire, of a Child in London".]

——, "Dylan Thomas", *The Atlantic Monthly*, CXCIII (February, 1954),
pp. 42-45. [Memories of Thomas as a youthful cherub and a sublime
reader; a discussion of "We lying by seasand"; a lament for Thomas's
early death.]

——, "Four New Poets", *London Mercury*, XXXIII (February, 1936), pp.
383-390. [A discussion of four new poets: William Empson, Ronald
Bottrall, Dylan Thomas, Archibald MacLeish.]

——, "The Love of Man, the Praise of God", *New York Herald Tribune Book
Review* (May 10, 1953), pp. 1, 14. [A review of *Collected Poems*.]

Slote, Bernice, and Miller, James E., Jr., "Of Monkeys, Nudes, and the Good
Gray Poet: Dylan Thomas and Walt Whitman", *Western Humanities
Review*, XIII (Autumn, 1959), pp. 339-353. [A comparison and contrast
of Whitman and Thomas as to language, emphasis, manner, theme, image,
etc.]

Smith, A. J., "The Art of the Intricate Image", *Letterature Moderne*, VII
(November-December, 1958), pp. 697-703. [A treatment which includes
a detailed analysis of "Our eunuch dreams".]

*Smith, William Jay, "Life, Literature, and Dylan", *Yale Literary Magazine*,
CXXII (November, 1954), p. 7. [Personal reminiscences of Thomas as man
and poet.]

Spacks, Patricia Meyer, "Thomas' 'In My Craft or Sullen Art,' 6-9", *Explicator*,
XVIII (December, 1959), item 21.

Spender, Stephen, "Dylan Thomas", *Britain Today*, No. 213 (January, 1954),
pp. 15-18. [A statement on the significance of Thomas's death.]

——, "Poetry for Poetry's Sake and Poetry Beyond Poetry", *Horizon*, XIII
(April, 1946), pp. 221-238. [A distinction between "transparent" and
"opaque" poetry; a discussion of Thomas's poetic virtues.]

——, "A Romantic in Revolt", *Spectator*, CLXXXIX (December 5, 1952), pp.
780-781. [A review of *Collected Poems* which Thomas himself praised as
"the clearest, most considered and sympathetic, and, in my opinion,
truest review that I have ever seen of my writing".]

Stearns, Marshall W., "Dylan Thomas's 'After the Funeral' ('In Memory of
Ann Jones')", *Explicator*, III (May, 1945), item 52.

*——, "Unsex the Skeleton: Notes on the Poetry of Dylan Thomas", *Sewanee
Review*, LII (July, 1944), pp. 424-440. An evaluation of Thomas as an
original poet and as an influence on his fellow poets.]

Sweeney, John L., "The Round Sunday Sounds", *New Republic*, CXXVIII
(April 6, 1953), pp. 24-25. [A review of *Collected Poems*.]

Symons, Julian, "Obscurity and Dylan Thomas", *Kenyon Review*, II (Winter,
1940), pp. 60-71. [An accusation that Thomas deliberately employs
obscurity of manner to hide the shallowness of his poetry's subject-matter.]

Tambimuttu, M. J., "First Letter", *Poetry* (London), I (February, 1939) [1-4].
[A statement of the purposes and principles of this new magazine; an

introduction to Thomas's "A saint about to fall", printed on pp. 26-27 of the issue.]

——, "Fourth Letter", *Poetry* (London), I (January 15, 1941), p. 90. [A commentary on an article, printed in this issue, by Pierre Jean Jouve; a reference to Thomas as an important pre-war poet.]

——, "Second Letter", *Poetry* (London), I (April, 1939) [2]. [A statement of the catholic nature of poetry accepted for publication in *Poetry*; a mention of Thomas in a comment on the existence of differences in literary opinion.]

Thomas, Caitlin, "Dylan Thomas and Emlyn Williams", *New Statesman and Nation*, XLIX (June 11, 1955), p. 815. [A commentary on Emlyn Williams's performance at the Globe Theatre of "A Boy Growing Up", a portrayal of the characters in Thomas's prose works.]

Thompson, Dunstan, "Time for Terror", *New Republic*, CII (April 1, 1940), pp. 447-448. [A review of *The World I Breathe*.]

Tindall, William York, "Burning and Crested Song", *American Scholar*, XXII (Autumn, 1953), pp. 486-490. [An explicative review of *Collected Poems*.]

——, "The Poetry of Dylan Thomas", *American Scholar*, XVII (Autumn, 1948), pp. 431-439. [An examination of Thomas's poetry when it was little known in America; an evaluation of Thomas as "the best and most magical English-speaking poet to have appeared since Yeats began to write".]

Treece, Henry, "Chalk Sketch for a Genius", *Dock Leaves*, V (Spring, 1954), pp. 18-23. [A sympathetic appraisal of Thomas's literary position, identical to sections i-iv of the "Introduction" to the 1956 edition of Treece's *Dylan Thomas: "Dog Among the Fairies"*.]

——, "Corkscrew or Footrule? Some Notes on the Poetry of Dylan Thomas", *Poetry* (London), I (May-June, 1941), pp. 196-199. [A discussion of various influences upon Thomas. Cf. the 1956 edition of Treece's *Dylan Thomas: "Dog Among the Fairies"*.]

Tyler, Parker, "Then Was My Neophyte a Scriptist", *Poetry*, LXXXVII (November, 1955), pp. 116-118. [A review of *The Doctor and the Devils*.]

Untermeyer, Louis, "Eight Poets", *Yale Review*, XXXIII (Winter, 1944), p. 351. [A review of *New Poems*.]

——, "Poet's Portrait as a Doomed Man", *Saturday Review*, XXXVIII (November 19, 1955), pp. 16-18. [A review of John Malcolm Brinnin's *Dylan Thomas in America*.]

Verschoyle, Derek, "Mr. Dylan Thomas", *Spectator*, CLXIV (April 5, 1940), p. 496. [A review of *Portrait of the Artist as a Young Dog*.]

"Verse", *New Yorker*, XXII (December 21, 1946), p. 99. [A review of *The Selected Writings of Dylan Thomas*, edited by John L. Sweeney.]

**Wain, John, "Dylan Thomas: A Review of his *Collected Poems*", in *Preliminary Essays* (New York, St. Martin's Press, 1957), pp. 180-185. [A criticism of Thomas's poetry on the basis that it is limited in subject-matter and is quasi-automatic.]

Wanning, Andrews, "Criticism and Principles: Poetry of the Quarter", *Southern Review*, VI (Spring, 1941), pp. 806-809. [An examination of "Twenty-four years" to illustrate the theory that Thomas's poetry has an intelligible unity generated by metaphor.]

Werry, Richard R., "The Poetry of Dylan Thomas", *College English*, XI (February, 1950), pp. 250-256. [A discussion of special characteristics of Thomas's poetic themes and craftsmanship.]

Williams, Raymond, "Dylan Thomas's Play for Voices", *Critical Quarterly*, I (Spring, 1959), pp. 18-26. [An analysis and appraisal of *Under Milk Wood*.]

Williams, William Carlos, "Dylan Thomas", *Yale Literary Magazine*, CXXII (November, 1954), pp. 21-22. [A commentary on Thomas as poet and prose writer.]

Wimsatt, William Kurtz, Jr., "Verbal Style: Logical and Counterlogical", *PMLA*, LXV (March, 1950), pp. 5-20. [A discussion of a level of meaning that is simultaneously related to but separable from the stated and substantial meaning.]

Zigerell, James, "Thomas' 'When All My Five and Country Senses See'", *Explicator*, XIX (November, 1960), item 11.

3. *Special Issues and Groups of Articles on Dylan Thomas*

Adam International Review, No. 238 (1953): A Dylan Thomas Number
The Editor, "For Dylan", ii-7.
Stravinsky, Igor, "The Opera that might have been", 8.
John, Augustus, "The monogamous bohemian", 9-10.
"Three first memoirs", 11-13.
    Lindsay, Philip, 11.
    Daiches, David, 12-13.
    Jones, Glyn, 13.
"Une larme pour Adonais", 13-14.
    Campbell, Roy, 13.
    Spender, Stephen, 14.
    Lehmann, John, 14.
    Litvinoff, Emmanuel, 14.
    Lutyens, Elizabeth, 14.
Barker, George, "A Swansong at Laugharne", 15-16.
Emmanuel, Pierre, "In Memoriam Dylan", 16.
Macleod, Runia Sheila, "The Dylan I knew", 17-23.
"Seventeen further memoirs", 24-39.
***   Johnson, Pamela Hansford, 24-25.
    Luzi, Mario, 25.
    Patmore, Derek, 25-26.
    Davenport, John, 26-27.
    His Publisher, 27-28.
    Manning, Hugo, 29.
    Dyment, Clifford, 29.
    Griffiths, William, 30.
    Pocock, Robert, 30-31.
    Marriott, R. B., 31-32.

Ayrton, Michael, 32.
Rees, Leslie, 33.
Wishart, Ralph, 33-34.
MacDiarmid, Hugh, 35.
Burton, Phillip, 36-37.
Price, Cecil, 37-39.
Williams, Griffith, 39.
Astie, Georges-Albert, "Victoire de la poésie", 40-42.
Deux Poèmes de Thomas, 42-43.
Huddlestone, Linden, "To take to give is all", 44-47.
Thomas, Dylan, "Adventures in the Skin Trade", 48-65.
*Roussillat, Suzanne, "His work and background", 66-72.
***Merwin, W[illiam] S., "The religious poet", 73-78.
Bottrall, Ronald, "The Sea", 78.
Etheridge, Ken, "Dylan Marlais Thomas", 79-80.
Portraits by Michael Ayrton and Alfred James.

Encounter, II (January, 1954)
"Dylan Thomas: Memories and Appreciations", 9-17.
***   I. Jones, Daniel. 9-10.
*   II. Roethke, Theodore. 11.
***   III. MacNeice, Louis. 12-13.
***   IV. Adix, Marjorie. 13-16.
*   V. Barker, George. 16-17.

Dock Leaves, V (Spring, 1954): A Dylan Thomas Number
Editorial
A Dylan Thomas Award
Lewis, Saunders, "Dylan Thomas", 8-9.
Davies, Aneirin Talfan, "The Golden Echo", 10-17.
Treece, Henry, "Chalk Sketch for a Genius", 18-23. [Identical to sections
    i, ii, iii, and iv in the introduction to the 1956 edition of Treece's
    Dylan Thomas: "Dog Among the Fairies".]
Jones, Glyn, "Dylan Thomas and Welsh", 24-25.
Prys-Jones, A. G., "Death Shall Have No Dominion", 26-29.
Mathias, Roland, "A Merry Manshape (or Dylan Thomas at a distance)",
    30-39.
Knowles, Suzanne and Peter Preece, "Poems", 17, 29.

Yale Literary Magazine, CXXII (November, 1954): A Dylan Thomas Number
Communications.
*Eberhart, Richard, "Some Memories of Dylan Thomas", 5-6.
Moore, Marianne, 6.
*Smith, William Jay, "Life, Literature, and Dylan", 7.
Deutsch, Babette, "For Dylan Thomas on the Day of His Death", 8.
Villa, Jose Garcia, "Death and Dylan Thomas", 9.
Harris, Marguerite, "Four Poems for Dylan Thomas", 10-12.
**Scott, Winfield Townley, "Death, and Some Dominions of It", 13-14.

Friar, Kimon, "Dylan Thomas and the Poetic Drama", 15-19.
Cummings, E. E. 19.
***Reid, Alastair, "A First Word", 20.
Williams, William Carlos, "Dylan Thomas", 21-22.
Gardner, Isabella, "When a Warlock Dies", 22.
Tusiani, Joseph, "For Dylan Thomas on the Day of His Death"
    (Translated from the Italian by Francis Winwar), 23-25.
Rexroth, Kenneth, "Lament for Dylan Thomas," 26-27.
Fowlie, Wallace, "On the Death of Dylan Thomas", 28-29.
**Gregory, Horace, "Romantic Heritage in the Writings of Dylan Thomas",
    30-34.

Poetry, LXXXVII (November, 1955), 63-129: A Dylan Thomas Number
Sitwell, Edith, "Elegy for Dylan Thomas", 63-67.
Thomas, Dylan, "Five Early Poems", 84-90.
    "Out of a War of Wits", 84-85.
    "This is Remembered", 85-86.
    "Shiloh's Seed", 87-89.
    "Before We Mothernaked Fall", 89-90.
    "The Almanac of Time", 90.
Photograph of Dylan Thomas, 91.
Reproductions of drafts for "Poem on His Birthday", 92-99.
***Shapiro, Karl, "Dylan Thomas", 100-110. [Appears not only in Tedlock
    and in Casebook, but also, in slightly altered phrasing, in Shapiro's
    In Defense of Ignorance (New York: Random House, 1960), pp.
    171-186.]
*Campbell, Roy, "Memories of Dylan Thomas at the B.B.C.", 111-114.
Lougée, David, "The Worlds of Dylan Thomas", 114-115.
    [A review of Quite Early One Morning and of Adventures in the Skin
    Trade and other Stories.]
Tyler, Parker, "Then Was My Neophyte a Scriptist", 116-118.
    [A review of The Doctor and the Devils.]
Ghiselin, Brewster, "Critical Work in Progress", 118-119.
    [A review of Elder Olson's The Poetry of Dylan Thomas.]
Baro, Gene, "The Orator of Llareggub", 119-122.
    [A review of Under Milk Wood.]